JOHN H. MINAN

KEVIN COLE

THE LITTLE
WHITE BOOK

of

BASEBALL
LAW

AMERICAN BAR ASSOCIATION
Defending Liberty
Pursuing Justice

12 11 10   6 5 4

Library of Congress Cataloging-in-Publication Data

John H. Minan
    The Little White Book of Baseball Law
    John H. Minan
Library of Congress Cataloging-in-Publication Data is on file.

ISBN: 978-1-60442-100-2

Dedication

This book is dedicated to the general manager of the Minan team, my wife Margo.

Table of Contents

ix   Foreword

xi   Preface

3   The First Inning:
Ticket Seller "Scalps" Police
Lainer v. City of Boston,
95 F. Supp. 2d 17 (D.Mass 2000)

15   The Second Inning:
Fantasy Baseball and Reality
CBC Distribution and Marketing, Inc. v.
Major League Baseball Advanced Media, L.P.,
505 F.3d. 818 (8th Cir. 2007), *cert. denied* (2008)

27   The Third Inning:
The Player in the Iron Mask
Thayer v. Spaulding, 27 F. 66 (CC. N.D. Ill. 1886)

39   The Fourth Inning:
MLB's Historical Antitrust Exemption
Federal Baseball Club of Baltimore v.
National League, 259 U.S. 200 (1922)

49   The Fifth Inning:
The Supreme Court "Balks" at
Changing the Antitrust Exemption
Flood v. Kuhn et al., 407 U.S. 258 (1972)

61   The Sixth Inning:
"Hey, Beerman!"
Donchez v. Coors Brewing Co.,
392 F.3d 1211 (10th Cir. 2004)

71 The Seventh Inning:
Ballpark Legal Warfare

Padres L.P. v. Henderson, 114 Cal. App.
4th 495 (2003), *rehearing denied* (2004)

87 The Eighth Inning:
Up for Grabs?

Alex Popov v. Patrick Hayashi,
2002 WL 31833731 (Cal. Superior)

107 The Ninth Inning:
**Stadium Liability
for Spectator Injuries**

Benejam v. Detroit Tigers, Inc., 246 Mich.
App. 645, 635 N.W.2d 219 (Mich. Ct. App. 2001)

117 The Tenth Inning:
**Liability for Negligent Medical
Assistance to Injured Spectators**

Fish v. Los Angeles Dodgers Baseball Club, et al.,
56 Cal. App. 3d 620, 128 Cal. Rptr. 807 (2d Dist. 1976)

129 The Eleventh Inning:
**Former MLB Players Argue
Reverse Discrimination**

Moran v. Selig, 447 F.3d 748 (9th Cir. 2006)

139 The Twelfth Inning:
**To Breach or Not to Breach:
That Is the Question**

*ESPN, Inc. v. Office of the Commissioner
of Baseball*, 76 F. Supp. 2d 383 (S.D.N.Y. 1999)

151 The Thirteenth Inning:
Pitcher Safety and Metal Bats
Sanchez v. Hillerich & Bradsby Co.,
104 Cal. App. 4th 703 (2002)

169 The Fourteenth Inning:
The "Beanball," "Brushback," or "Chin Music"
Avila v. Citrus Community College District,
41 Cal. Rprt. 3d 299 (2006)

183 The Fifteenth Inning:
**Stockpiling Trademarks
and the "Hall of Shame"**
*Central Manufacturing, Inc. v. George Brett
and Brett Bros.,* 492 F.3d 876 (7th Cir. 2007)

193 The Sixteenth Inning:
Umps Reverse Their Employment Call
*Major League Umpires Association v. American
League of Professional Baseball Clubs,* 357 F.3d 272
(3rd Cir. 2004), *cert. denied* (2005)

205 The Seventeenth Inning:
The "World Series" of Payroll Tax Litigation
*United States v. Cleveland Indians
Baseball Company,* 532 U.S. 200 (2001)

215 The Eighteenth Inning:
Fan Cries Foul
Jeffrey Swiecicki v. José Delgado,
463 F.3d 489 (6th Cir. 2006)

229 **About the Authors**

231 **Index**

Foreword

Many fans know the numerous "laws" of baseball, or the rules of thumb that have developed over the years and that govern coaches and players on the field. Batters should not embarrass pitchers by admiring a well-struck home run. Pitchers should not show up batters by celebrating too exuberantly after a strike out. Coaches can argue with umpires, but if they cross some unwritten lines they will be ejected.

Baseball has informal ways to enforce these "laws," too. Pitchers sometimes become disciplinarians: a four-seam fastball thrown just below the batter's chin is one remedy for baseball infractions, although this method can create problems of its own.

Some of these "laws" might be viewed as silly superstitions. For instance, it is bad luck for players and coaches to step on the foul lines when running on and off the field. But baseball's idiosyncratic "laws" are part of what makes the game special and what inspires obsessive devotion from millions of fans around the world.

Most fans—lawyers and non lawyers alike—know much less about baseball law, or the cases that have arisen and that affect the operation of baseball leagues, teams and other organizations. *The Little White Book of Baseball Law* is a useful primer on the subject for lawyers and even non lawyer fans, who are interested in learning more about how the law shapes the game we love.

Perhaps not surprisingly, some of the cases described in this book reflect the quirks of baseball, but many of them also deal with legal issues with which lawyers are familiar in other settings, such as labor and employment matters, real estate law, and antitrust issues.

I hope you will enjoy this book as a lawyer and as a fan.

William H. Neukom
Former President of the American Bar Association
and general managing partner and CEO
of the San Francisco Giants

Preface

The *Little White Book of Baseball Law* deals with life, baseball, and the law. The game of baseball has been America's beloved national pastime for over 150 years. As such, it enjoys a unique place in the American heritage. Baseball, which is avidly followed by millions, provides fans with a special source of inspiration and pride.

Although bookstores are filled with popular books about baseball, as well as those dealing with the law, *The Little White Book of Baseball Law* is one of a kind. To my knowledge no similar book exists.

The book tracks the real-life stories of people who journey through the legal system seeking justice. Their journeys through the halls of justice are divided into chapters called "innings." The eighteen stories were selected as a metaphor for a baseball "double header." Although many of the stories involve major league baseball (MLB), the common theme that unites the stories is the game of baseball generally.

The book is written to appeal to sports fans and lawyers alike. One does not have to be a lawyer or have legal training to enjoy it. The stories were chosen to stimulate the reader's imagination and curiosity. Because the stories center on legal disputes, the reader will encounter important and interesting legal principles along the way.

The cases are written in the short-story style favored by author William Sydney Porter, known to literature lovers as O. Henry.[1] The references to baseball history, songs, movies, and other asides are intended to add to the reader's enjoyment. Because the innings or chapters are independent stories, they may be read in any order without diminishing the enjoyable journey that lies ahead. As the reader will discover, some of baseball's heroes, as well as its rogues, make guest appearances throughout the book.

In some instances, the individual stories were selected because they have had a profound impact on the game. The cases decided by the U.S. Supreme Court fit within this category. In other instances, the cases were chosen because they raise typical legal issues, such as fan or player safety at the ballpark.

Some of the legal battles that lie ahead include the criminal liability of a fan charged with "scalping" baseball tickets outside a ballpark; the kerfuffle over the ownership of MLB statistics used in the billion-dollar business of fantasy baseball; an early patent infringement claim against the Spalding brothers over their illegal copying of the first catcher's mask, descriptively called the "rat trap"; the legal dustup between fans over the ownership of Barry Bonds's historic homerun ball; a malicious prosecution claim against the attorney at the center of the opposition

---

1. As an adult, Porter changed the spelling of his middle name given to him at birth from "Sidney" to "Sydney."

to the siting of a MLB ballpark; and a baseball stadium's liability for injury to spectators.

Also included are the Supreme Court's decisions on baseball's historical antitrust exemption, the Curt Flood antitrust reprise, and the "World Series" of payroll tax litigation between the Cleveland Indians and the Internal Revenue Service. For those readers partial to a frosty beer at the ballpark or elsewhere, the "Hey, Beerman" case may slake your thirst for enjoyment.

Each case was litigated either in a federal or state court. The actual judicial opinions accompanying the case often are lengthy and involve multiple legal issues as well as disputed factual matters. The official version may run 30 or more pages of single-spaced text. To capture core ideas, the stories simplify matters. Consequently, the shortened stories inevitably lack some of the detail and comprehensiveness of the full judicial opinion.

For those readers wanting to know more about any case, the name and official citation are given in the heading to each inning. The first footnote to each case gives the Web address where the opinion may be found on the internet. But the reader is forewarned. Web addresses are continually changing. If the reader cannot find the opinion at the address cited, it may have changed. If it has changed or none is given in the footnote, the full opinion is available through specialized legal data bases, such as Westlaw or LEXIS-NEXIS.

After each inning, my co-author discusses in the "Umpire's Rulings" some aspect of the Rules of Baseball that relates, more or less closely, to the case. The purpose is not to educate the true rules aficionado, like an umpire, or to provide definitive advice to be used in critical situations, such as resolving a bar bet. Rather, it is to highlight rules that might be interesting, but perhaps unknown, to the casual baseball fan. Many fans will be surprised by the complexity of the rules and by the varying approaches they take to different issues. It is possible to watch and enjoy baseball for years without appreciating their subtlety. The "Umpire's Rulings" reflect the wisdom accumulated during his years of coaching baseball, when he studied the rules with great care to increase his chances of winning arguments against "opposing counsel."

The book is not intended as a comprehensive exegesis on the law nor as a substitute for legal advice. The law is dynamic and continually changing. In addition, what may be law in one state is not necessarily the law in another. Finally, lawyers and judges frequently disagree on the meaning or interpretation of a particular case. This suggests that an actual legal problem concerning baseball should be discussed with a lawyer.

I am indebted to my friends and colleagues who have aided me with their comments, guidance, and support. I extend a special thanks to the following accomplished and dedicated lawyers—Michael Reed, James Sandler, and Gary Schons. Thanks also are extended to my colleagues at the University of San Diego School of Law (USD), Nancy Carol Carter and Teresa O'Rourke, and our friends at the National Baseball Hall of Fame and Museum, Jim Gates and Gabriel Schechter. Finally, my research assistants at USD deserve recognition for their able assistance and dedication. They include Robert Drakulich, Andrew Flior, executive editor of the USD *Law Review*, and Garret Wait.

As the humorist Dave Barry has quipped, baseball is a metaphor for life and the curve balls we face on the field of life:

> In life, as in baseball, we must leave the dugout of complacency, step up to the home plate of opportunity, adjust the protective groin cup of caution and swing the

bat of hope at the curve ball of fate, hoping that we can hit a line drive of success past the shortstop of misfortune, then sprint down the basepath of chance, knowing that at any moment we may pull the hamstring muscle of inadequacy and fall face-first onto the field of failure, where the chinch bugs of broken dreams will crawl into our nose.[2]

It is time to leave the "dugout of complacency" and head to the first inning.

The reader will ultimately be the umpire of whether the outcome of each inning is to be booed as "wild pitches" of legal legerdemain or cheered as good calls. One thing is certain. At the end of the 18th inning, the reader will not be surprised to learn that more legal disputes emerge from the sport of baseball than any other single sport.

John H. Minan
Professor of Law
University of San Diego School of Law
San Diego, CA 92110

---

2. Dave Barry, "Grab your pajamas, it's World Series time," MIAMI HERALD, Oct. 21, 2001. Also *available at* http://www.hereinstead.com/sys-tmpl/bbdavebarryonbaseball (last visited Oct. 26, 2008).

THE LITTLE
WHITE BOOK

of

BASEBALL
LAW

WDFA03 104
2
15
RESERVED WDFA03
$50.00
X9Z2212
SCTN 104
THE BIG GAME
FA03 104
2
15
RESERVED WDFA03
$50.00
X9Z2212
SCTN 104
ROW 2
SEAT 15
THE BIG GAME
CENTRAL STADIUM
OCTOBER 1, 2008 6PM

Ticket Seller "Scalps" Police

Lainer v. City of Boston,
95 F. Supp. 2d 17 (D. Mass 2000)

"Get Your Tickets Here!"

"Ticket scalping" involves reselling a ticket, usually by a speculator, for more than the ticket is worth. It should be distinguished from the resale of tickets through a licensed broker at prices greater than the face value of the ticket. These licensed resales may not violate anti-scalping laws.

The practice of ticket scalping usually occurs when there is a high demand for tickets to a ball game. The prized ticket may be for opening day, where the hopes and dreams for the season lie ahead, for a regular season game against a fierce rival, or for a divisional playoff game or the World Series.

The practice of markets developing to meet demand outside the official distribution channels is long-standing. On April 18, 1923, for example, two enterprising entrepreneurs were hawking tickets to the Yankees-Boston Red Sox game at the new Yankee Stadium, which would become known as the "House That Ruth Built."[1] One was asking $1.25 for his ticket, which was 15 cents

---

1. The "Babe" hit a home run to give the Yankees a 4–1 victory over the Sox.

more than the official ticket price. The other was asking $1.50. Both were busted by the police for scalping. Creative baseball marketing methods develop to meet demand. Tickets are available through Web sites such as Stub-Hub, Craigslist, and eBay. The Chicago-based company First-Dibz.com started selling the right to purchase tickets during the summer of 2008 "should" the Chicago Cubs make the World Series in the fall of 2008, which they did not. The Web site advertised: "For the first time ever, Cubs season ticket holders can now sell the 'rights' to their Playoff tickets. EVEN IF THE GAMES ARE NEVER PLAYED, you can make money!"[2] The company takes a 17 percent service charge for the transaction. But major league baseball (MLB) owners are not likely to suffer such turf intrusions in silence.[3]

Traditional sources for tickets include "entrepreneurs" selling them near or outside the baseball stadiums. Most fans are familiar with sellers frantically waving tickets at those passing by or yelling "get your tickets here." Although the practice may be common, such ticket resale also may be illegal.

Generalizations about the practice of reselling of tickets are difficult to accurately state, because the law varies so much. Some states place no restrictions on resale, but others place

---

2. *Available at* http://www.firstdibz.com/index.action (last visited July 22, 2008). The Cubs' run to the 2008 World Series was cut short, so accessing this site may be problematic.

Section 1.5(a) of the Illinois Ticket Scalping Act provides that "it is unlawful for any person, persons, firm or corporation to sell tickets for baseball games . . . for a price more than the price printed upon the face of said ticket, and the price of said ticket shall correspond with the same price shown at the box office or the office of original distribution." 720 ILL. COMP. STATE. ANN. 375/1.5(a) (West 2002). Although Section 1.5(a) of the Ticket Scalping Act prohibits the sale of tickets at more than face value, section 1.5(b) delineates exceptions to the general prohibition, which does not apply to ticket brokers duly registered with the Illinois Office of the Secretary of State.

3. In 2006, New York Yankees season-ticket holders who were suspected of reselling their regular-season seats on StubHub received letters denying them the right to buy playoff tickets and barring them from buying season tickets for the 2007 season.

restrictions on the amount charged for the ticket, the place of the resale, compliance with broker-licensing requirements, and so on. The legality of the practice also may be affected by local ordinances. California, for example, allows municipalities to impose additional restrictions that go beyond the state law restriction that prohibits resale above the face value of the ticket.[4] Therefore, local law also may apply.

The regulation of ticket resale is justified by state or local government on a variety of theories. It arguably exists to prevent fraud, extortion, exorbitant demands, and other abuses that conflict with the public welfare. Counterfeit tickets are a reality.

In addition to publicly imposed restrictions, such as licensing sellers, the law allows the event sponsor issuing the ticket to impose reasonable conditions on the initial purchaser. The event sponsor may prohibit or otherwise restrict the transfer of the ticket to another party. In order to give notice to the initial purchaser, the conditions and restrictions for admission usually are printed on the ticket. The printed notice may state, for example, that the ticket is a "personal license, which is not transferable, and may not be resold or offered for resale at a premium."[5]

---

4. People v. Shepard, 141 Cal. Rptr. 379 (Cal. Ct. App.1977), *cert. denied*, 436 U.S. 917 (1978) (upholding the misdemeanor conviction of a ticket seller for violating a local ordinance which, in effect, prohibited all such sales on the stadium premises, and finding that the ordinance was not preempted by a state statute prohibiting ticket scalping).
California Penal Code, Section 346, provides:

Any person who, without the written permission of the owner or operator of the property on which an entertainment event is to be held or is being held, sells a ticket of admission to the entertainment event, which was obtained for the purpose of resale, at any price which is in excess of the price that is printed or endorsed upon the ticket, while on the grounds of or in the stadium, arena, theater, or other place where an event for which admission tickets are sold is to be held or is being held, is guilty of a misdemeanor.

5. *See, e.g.*, Levine v. Brooklyn Nat'l League Baseball Club, Inc., 36 N.Y.S.2d 474(N.Y. Sup. Ct. 1942) (holding a ticket to a place of amusement is merely a revocable license, and the right of the defendant to make the conditions printed on its tickets, and to refuse all tickets transferred in violation thereof, cannot be questioned).

Fan Bites Back

Lainer is interesting because it presents an unusual twist on the typical ticket-scalping story. It is somewhat of a "fan bites back" case.

On Saturday, July 31, 1999, Gary Lainer and some friends planned on going to Boston's "Elysian Fields," Fenway Park, to see a game between the Red Sox and the New York Yankees. This ongoing rivalry recently received worldwide attention. Trying to outdo the "Curse of the Bambino," a construction worker attempted to start a new jinx on the Bronx Bombers by burying a Red Sox shirt in the new Yankee Stadium, which was then under construction and set to open in 2009. The prank was discovered and the shirt was removed in 2008.

Because a friend who intended to go to the game with Gary couldn't make the game at the last minute, Gary had an extra ticket to the grandstand. He had bought the ticket for $18. Not wanting to be stuck with the ticket, he walked along the street just outside Fenway Park calling out "anyone need a ticket?"

Gary found a buyer. He asked the buyer for the face value of the ticket. The buyer gave him a $20 bill for the ticket and Gary attempted to give the buyer $2 in change. According to Gary, things quickly went awry. He was grabbed by two cops, punched from behind in his right kidney area, and arrested. Gary then was hauled off to the police station, booked, photographed, fingerprinted, and, for good measure, "chained to a wall," presumably to prevent his escape to his Massachusetts veterinary practice.

Gary was charged with violating Massachusetts's anti-scalping statute, hawking and peddling without a license, and "occupying a public way without a license" in violation of a local Boston ordinance. After cooling his heels for two-and-a-half hours at the police station, he was released on his own recognizance after agreeing to appear in court several days later. His ticket to the game was confiscated as "evidence," so Gary also missed the game.

Thereafter, Gary appeared in court as required, and was charged with the above "high" crimes. Following several hours of waiting, during which the wheels of justice ground away, the charges were finally and inexplicably dismissed. But the city of Boston had not heard the last of veterinarian Gary Lainer.

Gary sued the city of Boston, the commissioner of the Boston Police Department (BPD), and three of its officers. He claimed they had violated his constitutional rights and he wanted injunctive relief against the BPD for its erroneous enforcement of Massachusetts law and damages for his unlawful arrest.

The core to his complaint was the BPD's long-standing policy of "arresting any person that attempts to sell or transfer Boston Red Sox tickets outside Fenway Park, regardless of the price charged." This automatic arrest policy and practice by the BPD, he argued, violated the Massachusetts anti-scalping law. In short, it was wrongly applying the law.

The Boston Police Department Policy

As stated in its enforcement manual, the BPD's arrest policy was clear. Any person reselling game tickets, for any amount, in a public area was subject to arrest. As evidence that the policy was enforced consistently with the manual, Gary submitted affidavits from several individuals who had been arrested under similar circumstances, as well as articles from the *Boston Globe* newspaper recounting stories of fans who had been arrested for attempting to sell or even give away tickets. In every instance, the person was arrested, charged, and forced to appear in court, only to have the charges dismissed with the imposition of court costs against the defendants. The action was more than an annoyance. It cost the arrested folks time and had a financial impact because they had to pay court costs.

The court found:

> In all of the various accounts, not a single individual was questioned as to whether they were in the business of selling tickets, or whether they possessed a license to sell tickets. Each was arrested solely on the basis of an attempt to sell or give away tickets, and all charges were eventually dismissed.

The Massachusetts Anti-Scalping Law

Those were the facts, but what about the law? The Massachusetts anti-scalping law, section 185A, states that "[n]o person shall engage in the business of reselling any ticket . . . without being licensed . . . by the commissioner of public safety." The requirement that the person be in "the business of reselling" is clearly stated. Therefore, the critical legal question is whether the circumstances of the arrest suggest that the person was in "the business of reselling" the ticket.

The city argued that "any" sale is a commercial transaction that constitutes the business of reselling. The court was not persuaded. If "any" sale triggered the application of the prohibition, the court reasoned that the legislature would not have included the language "in the business." It would have said "any resale." But the statute precludes resale of tickets only when done in the course of business without a license.

The city also argued that "none of the potential plaintiffs are permitted to resell their tickets by the Boston Red Sox." This claim also was rejected because, whatever the Red Sox's ticket policy, it has no bearing on a person's right to be free from wrongful arrest. Thus, the evidence indicates that Gary did not violate Massachusetts law and that he was wrongfully arrested.

The Umpire's Call

The court granted the motion for a preliminary injunction:

> Defendants, and all of their officers, agents, servants, employees, attorneys and those persons in active concert or participation with them, from attempting to arrest, threatening to arrest, arresting, and prosecuting any person who attempts to resell or resells any ticket to a Boston Red Sox baseball game in the vicinity of Fenway Park, at or below the face value of the ticket, unless they have probable cause, at the time of arrest, to believe that said person is a person engaged in the business of reselling tickets, and is not duly licensed as required by Mass. Gen. Laws ch. 140, § 185A.

Next Up

The state statute, Section 185A, regulates the resale of tickets as a business venture, requiring individuals to obtain a license before engaging in that practice. The case does not stand for the proposition that a person has to make an actual sale or, at the other extreme, make multiple sales before being engaged in the business of selling. Trying to sell the ticket may be enough.

In addition, charging a price above the face value of a ticket may be consistent with and evidence of being in the business of selling. Once the licensing provision applies, Section 185D on service charges applies. It provides:

> No licensee under [§ 185A] shall resell any ticket . . . to any . . . public amusement or exhibition of any descrip-

tion at a price in excess of two dollars in advance of the price printed on the face of such tickets . . . as the purchase price thereof; provided, however, that a price in excess of the above maximum shall not be deemed in violation of this section if the amount in excess of the above maximum is solely attributable to service charges. For the purpose of this section, service charges are defined as costs incurred by said licensee related solely to the procuring and selling of such ticket . . . and not related to the general business operation of said licensee. Service charges include, but are not limited to, charges for messengers, postage, and long distance telephone calls, extensions of credit and costs attributable thereto. The imposition of a fee, on an annual or per order basis, for customers purchasing tickets other than by immediate payment therefor in cash, which includes a membership fee, office expenses and the cost of processing credit card orders, shall not be deemed a violation of this section.

In a 2008 Massachusetts case, Admit One was sued for violating Section 185D.[6] Since 2000, Admit One had been a licensed ticket reseller, and had advertised itself as the "largest Red Sox ticket agency nationwide." In 2005, it purchased 1,128 Red Sox tickets for resale from an unknown source.

In 2005, Colman Herman asked for price quotes from Admit One for loge-section seats for a series of games between the Red Sox and the New York Yankees and for a series between the Red Sox and the Baltimore Orioles. He was told that such seats for the Yankees games cost $500 and those for the Orioles games cost $165. He then asked what the face value of the tickets was, and was told "about $85." He did not buy the tickets.

Colman did send, however, a demand letter to Admit One's principal, claiming that "the prices quoted to me were exorbitant" and arguing that Admit One had violated the licensing provisions in Massachusetts law. Admit One responded by denying the violations and arguing that Colman had suffered no injury. In short, Colman had no legal standing to challenge Admit One on the theory of "no harm, no foul."

The court agreed, and dismissed the complaint. The statute requires the "reselling" of tickets at prices above those delineated. Without a transfer of property (the ticket) from one person to another, there was no sale. To apply the statute to offers to sell would be to expand the scope of the statute beyond that intended by the legislature.

---

6. Herman v. Admit One, 2008 Mass. App. Div. 125 (Mass. Dist. Ct. 2008).

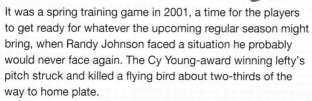

Umpire's Ruling

A Scalping Veterinarian and a Scalped Bird

It was a spring training game in 2001, a time for the players to get ready for whatever the upcoming regular season might bring, when Randy Johnson faced a situation he probably would never face again. The Cy Young-award winning lefty's pitch struck and killed a flying bird about two-thirds of the way to home plate.

The rules of baseball cover offensive, defensive, spectator, and umpire interference, but not avian interference. Accordingly, the umpire invoked Rule 9.01(c), which permits the umpire to use "common sense and fair play" to resolve points not specifically covered in the rules. The umpire ruled the play "no pitch,"[1] so Johnson got a do-over. The bird was not so lucky.

Consider a slightly different situation. During the rain-soaked first day of the final game of the 2008 World Series, a bird was caught by television cameras walking in fair territory near the first-base line. (Perhaps it was looking for worms.) What would have happened if a batted ball had struck the bird?

For major league umpires, the official rules are supplemented by additional regulations. While they did not refer to pitched balls striking an animal at that time, they did cover batted and thrown balls (other than pitches). The ball is considered alive and in play as if it had not touched the animal.[2]

One wonders whether the umpire in the Johnson incident gave consideration to the regulations applying to batted and thrown balls. Why one would treat these situations differently is not immediately apparent. Perhaps the answer is that it was spring training for the umpires too.[3]

---

1. RALPH NELSON, ASK THE UMPIRE, *available at* http://mlb.mlb.com/mlb/official_info/umpires/feature.jsp?feature=qa1.

2. *Id.*

3. However, the regulations now include a provision ratifying the result reached in the Johnson incident.

Fantasy Baseball and Reality

CBC Distribution and Marketing, Inc. v. Major League Baseball Advanced Media, L.P., 505 F.3d. 818 (8th Cir. 2007), cert. denied (2008)

"Am I Just Dreaming?"

Baseball[1] fantasies are common. Pitchers fantasize about pitching the perfect game,[2] fielders dream of turning the unassisted triple play,[3] and fans and players imagine their team winning the World Series. The film classic, *Field of Dreams* (1989), is a fantasy that explores America's love affair with baseball. For some time after its release, the memorable words "If you build it, he will come" became almost as well known to baseball fans as the famous phrase "Say it ain't so, Joe,"[4] a phrase allegedly spoken by a young fan to "Shoeless" Joe Jackson as the 1919 "Black Sox" scandal unfolded.

---

1. The word "base-ball" first appeared in 1744. In 1817, "base ball" became two words without the hyphen. The conventional spelling "baseball" is reported to have appeared in 1817.

2. An official perfect game occurs when a pitcher (or pitchers) retires each batter on the opposing team without a batter reaching base during the course of the game.

3. A triple play is a play by the defense in which three offensive players are put out as a result of continuous action, providing there is no error between putouts.

4. After the bribe was discovered, a small boy is reported to have approached "Shoeless" Joe Jackson and exclaimed, "Say it ain't so, Joe." CHICAGO HERALD & EXAMINER, Sept. 30, 1920.

In *Field of Dreams*, the ghostly voice of "Shoeless" Joe Jackson[5] (Ray Liotta) encourages Ray Kinsella (Kevin Costner) to build a baseball diamond in his cornfield. Shoeless Joe was a member of the infamous White Sox baseball team that threw the 1919 World Series.[6] He asks Ray to build the baseball field to "ease his pain."

As the fantasy unfolds, Ray travels to Boston to see author Terence Mann (James Earl Jones) to discover the meaning of the voices and the purpose for the field. Mann tells him of the importance of baseball and its history:

> The one constant through all the years, Ray, has been baseball. America has rolled by like an army of steamrollers. It's been erased like a blackboard, rebuilt, and erased again. But baseball has marked the time. This field, this game, is a part of our past, Ray. It reminds us of all that once was good, and that could be again. Oh people will come, Ray. People will most definitely come.

Ray builds his fantasy ball field, complete with bleachers and floodlights, in the middle of an Iowa cornfield. The ghosts of Shoeless Joe[7] and other Sox players who were disgraced in the 1919 World Series scandal come back from the dead and, seek-

---

5. "Shoeless" Joe Jackson got his nickname during a game with the Brandon Mill team. Jackson suffered foot blisters from a new pair of cleats. They hurt him so much that he took his shoes off before batting. Once on base, a fan started yelling Jackson was a "Shoeless son of a gun." The nickname stuck like pine tar.

6. In this episode of baseball history, Abe Attell, supposedly an employee of New York gambler Arnold Rothstein, bribed eight Chicago White Sox players to throw the first and second games of the 1919 World Series to the Cincinnati Reds. The players, including "Shoeless" Joe Jackson, were indicted on charges of conspiracy to defraud the public for their participation in the scheme. All eight were acquitted. Nevertheless, major league baseball's first commissioner, Kenesaw Mountain Landis, banished the eight from baseball to shore up the game's image. In doing so, Landis tarred them with the sobriquet the "Black Sox."

7. Controversy abounds as to whether Jackson actually took part in throwing the Series, as he hit .375, with no fielding errors, against the Reds.

16

ing redemption from the scandal, appear for a few games with Ray. The story is a tribute to both the imagination and the glories of baseball.

Unlike the retrospective portrayed in *Field of Dreams*, fantasy baseball looks to the future. It has revolutionized the way fans view and participate in the game. But fantasy baseball has also created new legal headaches.

Before the baseball season begins each spring, participants form fantasy baseball teams by "drafting" current players from major league baseball (MLB) teams. Using one of the many Web sites available to host the fantasy league,[8] participants become the team owners of their assembled players. As the actual baseball season unfolds, participants compete against other fantasy baseball "owners" who have also drafted fantasy teams. A participant's success depends on the actual performance of the fantasy team's major league players. The object is to predict how the major league players will perform during the upcoming baseball season.

Many fantasy leagues are played for prize money, which is generated by entry and associated fees. Fantasy baseball is big business and it has revived interest and attracted new fans. More than six million people play fantasy baseball, and one 2005 estimate placed the economic impact at more than $1 billion. With this much money involved, legal disputes were predictable.

Fantasy Baseball Litigation

CBC Distribution and Marketing sells fantasy sports products. It incorporates the names of major league baseball players, along with performance and biographical data, through its Internet

---

8. Some of the more popular sites are sports.yahoo.com/fantasy; sportsline.com/fantasy; games.espn.go.com; and fanball.com.

Web site, e-mail, snail-mail, and the telephone. Participants in CBC's fantasy baseball games pay fees to play and additional fees to trade players during the course of the season. From 1995 through 2004, things went smoothly. CBC used the names and information about major league players under a license agreement with the MLB Players' Association (MLBPA). The agreements were entered into in 1995 and 2002. The 2002 agreement with the MLBPA, which superseded the 1995 agreement, licensed to CBC "the names, nicknames, likenesses, signatures, pictures, playing records, and/or biographical data of each player" for use in association with CBC's fantasy baseball products.

After the 2002 agreement with CBC expired in 2005, the MLBPA changed "players." It licensed to Major League Baseball Advanced Media, L.P. (Advanced Media) the exclusive right to use baseball players' names and performance information "for exploitation via all interactive media." Advanced Media then began providing fantasy baseball games at MLB.com, the official Web site of major league baseball. Through this arrangement, Advanced Media secured the "right" to use the names and performance information.

Advanced Media offered CBC the opportunity, in exchange for a commission, to promote the MLB.com fantasy baseball games on CBC's Web site. It did not offer CBC, however, a license to continue to offer its own fantasy baseball products. This proffered restructuring placed CBC's business model in jeopardy.

As a result, CBC filed suit in the Federal District Court for the Eastern District of Missouri. CBC alleged that it had "a reasonable apprehension that it will be sued by Advanced Media if it continues to operate its fantasy baseball games." It asked for a declaratory judgment against Advanced Media to establish its

18

right to use, without being licensed, the names and information about major league baseball players in connection with its fantasy baseball products.

Advanced Media filed a counterclaim. It argued CBC's fantasy baseball products violated the rights of publicity that belonged to major league baseball players. The players, through their association, had licensed those rights to Advanced Media, the interactive media and Internet company of major league baseball. The players association intervened in the suit, joining in Advanced Media's claims and further asserting a breach of contract claim against CBC.

Because no factual issues were in dispute, the federal district court granted summary judgment to CBC. Advanced Media and the players association appealed to the U.S. Court of Appeals for the Eighth Circuit. The appellate court reviewed *de novo* the district court's interpretation of Missouri law, including the interpretation of the right of publicity.

The Right of Publicity

The right of publicity is a relatively new type of intellectual property right that is a product of state law, not federal law. The Eighth Circuit was required, therefore, to apply Missouri law. In Missouri, a right of publicity action includes the following elements: (1) That defendant used the plaintiff's name as a symbol of his or her identity (2) without consent (3) and with the intent to obtain a commercial advantage.

The parties to the litigation agreed that the players' names and playing information were being used without consent, so this element was satisfied. The appellate court then turned to the other requirements: "symbol-of-identity" and "commercial advantage."

The appellate court relied on a prior decision by the Missouri Supreme Court that established the principle that the appropriation of an identity, in most cases, can be accomplished through the use of a person's name or likeness. Although the person whose identity is used may be identified by a real name, nickname, or professional name, the identity must be understood or recognized by the intended audience. The appellate court had no difficulty concluding that the symbol-of-identity requirement was met because the names of the professional players used by CBC and its subscribers knowingly referred to actual major league players.

The commercial advantage requirement was more difficult to find because CBC's use did not fit neatly into the more traditional commercial advantage categories, such as using the names of the major league players for advertising or product merchandising. There was nothing in the record to indicate that any MLB player was associated with CBC's games or that any player endorsed or sponsored the fantasy games. Moreover, the use of MLB names and playing statistics was not intended to draw customers away from other fantasy game providers because all fantasy game providers use the same names and playing records.

Notwithstanding these difficulties, the appellate court found that Missouri's commercial advantage element was also met. The court focused on the intent of CBC to secure a commercial benefit from the identities. Because it was using the baseball players' identities in its fantasy baseball products for purposes of making a profit, the court found that sufficient evidence existed to make out a cause of action for their rights of publicity. The fact that Advanced Media had a legally recognized right-of-publicity interest was not, however, the end of the ongoing game of "hard ball" before the appellate court.

The First Amendment

The appellate court next turned to reconciling the tension between the First Amendment rights of baseball fans and the baseball players' right of publicity. CBC argued that it had a constitutional right to use the baseball players' names, without being licensed, in connection with its fantasy baseball products. The appellate court agreed. It offered three reasons to support its conclusion.

First, the information used in CBC's fantasy baseball games is readily available in the public domain. Anyone could pick up a newspaper or other reference source and get the relevant player information. The court reasoned that "it would be strange law that a person would not have a First Amendment right to use information that is available to everyone."

Second, the court recognized the public value of information about baseball and its players. After all, baseball is widely seen as America's "national pastime." The records and statistics are of interest to the public because they allow fans to better appreciate (or often argue about) a player's performance. This baseball information, which is of substantial interest to the public, is a form of expression entitled to constitutional protection.

Finally, the court reasoned that "the facts in this case barely, if at all, implicate the interests that states typically intend to vindicate by providing rights of publicity to individuals." The economic interests that states seek to promote through the right of publicity include the right of an individual to reap the economic rewards of his or her endeavors. Other reasons for recognizing a publicity right are the desire to provide incentives to encourage a person's productive activities and to protect consumers from misleading advertising.

But, the court reasoned, MLB players are already handsomely rewarded for their participation in the game and may also earn additional monies from endorsements and sponsorship arrangements. Moreover, no danger exists that consumers will be misled. Fantasy baseball games do not create the false impression that some particular player with "star power" is endorsing CBC's products.

The appellate court held that, on balance, CBC's First Amendment rights in offering its fantasy baseball products supersede the players' rights of publicity. Therefore, it did not address CBC's alternative argument that federal copyright law preempts the players' state law rights of publicity.

The Players Association Contract Claim

Advanced Media and the MLBPA argued that CBC violated the 2002 license agreement. This agreement between the MLBPA and CBC specifically provided, "It is understood and agreed that [the Players Association] is the sole and exclusive holder of all right, title and interest in and to the Rights." This provision, it was argued, was an admission of their entitlement.

Although the parties did not cite to it in their briefs, the court found that the 2002 agreement contained "a warranty of title," which is defined as an assurance by one party to a contract of the existence of a fact upon which the other party may rely. Section 8(a) of the 2002 agreement provides that the MLBPA "is the sole and exclusive holder of all right, title and interest" in and to the names and playing statistics of virtually all major league baseball players. This representation warrantied that the MLBPA owned the publicity rights.

The court found that the MLBPA did not have the exclusive "right, title and interest" in the use of such information. The

MLBPA, therefore, breached a material contractual obligation. As a result of this breach, CBC was relieved of the obligations that it undertook under the agreement.

Strike Three

In February 2008, MLB, Advanced Media, and the MLBPA asked the U.S. Supreme Court to review the Eighth Circuit's decision.[9] They claimed that the court had misapplied the First Amendment. The Supreme Court refused to hear the case and did so without comment. One editorial shouted "Justices reject MLB's illogic, shameless greed."

The Court let stand the decision that gives for-profit fantasy leagues the right to continue operating without paying a licensing fee. Although as a technical matter the refusal to hear the case is not a decision of the merits, MLB and the MLPBA seem to have struck out in the attempt to get more money from baseball fans.

CBC's First Amendment rights trumped the state law right of publicity. Its constitutional right to use the players' names and statistical information took precedence over the players' rights to be protected from unauthorized publicity under Missouri law. In addition, The MLPBA could not enforce the no-use and no-challenge provisions of the 2002 agreement.

---

9. Brief for Petitioner-Appellant, Major League Baseball Advanced Media v. CBC Distribution and Marketing, Inc., 128 S. Ct. 2872 (2008) (No. 07-1099), 2008 WL 2061372.

Umpire's Ruling

The Limits of Free Expression

The First Amendment right to free expression that precluded legal sanctions against fantasy baseball leagues forbids only *governmental* punishment of speech. But the umpire is not the state, so players, managers, and coaches are subject to punishment (by ejection from the game and accompanying fines from the league) for engaging in certain prohibited speech.

Lawyers are familiar with the sometimes difficult distinction between fact and law, and a similar distinction is drawn in the Rules of Baseball: A manager can "appeal" an umpire's decision if there is "reasonable doubt" that the decision "may be in conflict with the rules," but a decision "which involves judgment, such as, but not limited to, whether a batted ball is fair or foul, whether a pitch is a strike or a ball, or whether a runner is safe or out, is final. No player, manager, coach or substitute shall object to any such judgment decisions." Of course, in many cases, the umpire will listen to some grousing about a judgment call, but such judgment calls cannot be the subject of an official protest.

The umpire's judgment on the strike zone is specially insulated from argument under the rules:

> Players leaving their position in the field or on base, or managers or coaches leaving the bench or coaches box, to argue on BALLS AND STRIKES will not be permitted. They should be warned if they start for the plate to protest the call. If they continue, they will be ejected from the game.[1]

This rule is an understandable limitation, given the frequent opportunity for differences of opinion on these calls, and the delay to the game if even a few of these opportunities became occasions for debate. However, "[T]he manager or the catcher may request the plate umpire to ask his partner for help on a half swing when the plate umpire calls the pitch a ball, but not

when the pitch is called a strike." The dispute in these cases falls on the fact side of the law/fact divide—it is not about whether the umpire knows the rules, but about how far the bat has traveled. This exception apparently recognizes that the plate umpire often lacks a good view to make this call and the appeal to the base umpire can be made quickly and without a conference.

Even when the manager has the right to appeal a decision, the manager must avoid "unsportsmanlike conduct or language," which is an independent ground for ejection. Certain "magic words" reputedly will guarantee ejection from the game, but they are neither listed in the rules nor included in this book.

---

1. Rule 9.02(a) Comment.

The Player in the Iron Mask

Thayer v. Spaulding, 27 F. 66 (CC. N.D. Ill. 1886)

The catcher arguably plays the toughest position in baseball.[1] In addition to hours of squatting and doing repetitive deep knee bends, the catcher is regularly forced to cope with numerous hazards of the game, including errantly pitched balls, foul tips, flying and broken bats, and opposing players charging at him at breakneck speed as they make for home plate. Today's catcher wears an array of protective equipment popularly called the "tools of ignorance."

In the early days of baseball, the catcher had no equipment to protect himself against such potential assaults. The catcher's "safety mask" was an important first step toward protecting his face from injury.

The catcher's "safety mask" was not, however, uniformly applauded by early purists of the game. One sportswriter, who could have played for the Luddites, wrote "there is about as much sense in putting a lightning rod on a catcher as there is a mask."

---

1. In his book, *Just Play Ball*, Joe Garagiola described the job this way: "If a catcher were asked to march in a parade they'd make him march behind the elephants. He'd have the same lousy view the whole parade and get dumped on at the same time. Think of it that way and it's easy to understand that even Charlie Brown's catcher would rather play the piano." Ironically, the numbering system used in baseball to identify a player's position assigns the catcher the number 2.

Although today's catcher's mask has evolved into something
Darth Vader could love, its function is the same as the earliest
mask—to protect the face of the catcher. The first catcher's
mask was invented by Fred W. Thayer, who patented his safety
innovation on February 12, 1878.[2] At first, Thayer's "better
mouse trap" was derisively described by some as a "rat trap,"
because it looked somewhat like one. But the idea of a mask was
sound, and it caught on with catchers.[3]

The mask also caught the attention of entrepreneurs. In
1877, Albert Goodwill Spalding,[4] a former pitcher with the Chicago
White Stockings and a major force in establishing the National
League, and his brother, J. Walter Spalding, started a business
to manufacture and sell sporting goods. A.G. Spalding & Bros.
subsequently grew into one of the most recognized names in the
manufacturing and selling of sports equipment.

While imitation may be the most sincere form of flattery,
Thayer didn't take kindly to the Spalding brothers' copying his

---

2. Ernest L. Thayer is recognized as the author of "Casey at the Bat." It first appeared in the *San Francisco Examiner* on June 3, 1888, subtitled "A Ballad of the Republic, Sung in the Year 1888." The relationship between Fred W. Thayer and Ernest L. Thayer is not known.

3. Masks have also caught on with musicians. Consider the lyrics to Fleetwood Mac's new song, "Make Me a Mask."

> *Make me a mask*
> *That I can wear*
> *Till day is done*
> *The wind in the trees*
> *The falling leaves*
> *The world's spinning*
> *Make me a mask*
> *So I can laugh*
> *Till nighttime comes*
> *No more can I stay*
> *How long must I play*
> *This game of winning . . . .*

4. Spalding created the first official baseball for the major leagues in the United States in 1876. Spalding's evolved version of that ball is now the official baseball of the National and American Leagues.

patented safety mask. Thayer sued the enterprising brothers for patent infringement in *Thayer v. Spaulding.*

The title or caption for the case, as well as the repeated references in the court's opinion, mistakenly refer to "Spaulding." This spelling error is attributable to the case reporter, Charles C. Linthicum of the Chicago Bar, who added an extra "u" to Spalding's name.

Name confusion in baseball is nothing new. In fact, it was raised to an art form by Bud Abbott and Lou Costello in the late 1930s and early 1940s. Their classic baseball comedy routine, "Who's on First," is premised on the confusion associated with using player names.[5]

Patent Law Principles

The U.S. Constitution authorizes Congress to establish a patent system to promote the progress of science and useful arts by giving authors and inventors the exclusive right to their respective writings and discoveries for a limited time. Pursuant to this authority, Congress has established a statutory system for the issuance and protection of patents. A federal patent gives the patentee the right to prevent others from making, using, or selling the patented invention without the patent holder's consent. It is the grant of a limited monopoly on the invention. Patents are now protected from infringement by federal law for a period of 20 years from the date of filing, not issuance.

To get a patent, the applicant must apply to the U.S. Patent and Trademark Office. The patent application must describe the

---

5. The names used in the comedy routine for the players at each position were: First Base: "Who"; Second Base: "What"; Third Base: "I Don't Know"; Leftfield: "Why"; Centerfield: "Because"; Pitcher: "Tomorrow"; Catcher: "Today"; and Shortstop: "I Don't Give a Darn!" The video can be seen at http://www.video.google.com/videoplay?docid=-8342445135331678445. In 1999, *Time* magazine named "Who's on First?" the Best Comedy Sketch of the Twentieth Century, and in 2005, the line "Who's on First?" was included on the American Film Institute's list of 100 memorable movie quotes.

invention by written specification. This specification is a critical part of the patent process because it gives the public, as well as the patentee, notice as to what is protected. The written specification typically consists of various standard parts, such as a background, a summary, and one or more claims, which delineate the elements and limitations to the invention.

To be patentable, the invention must be distinguishable from the prior art by being both novel[6] and non-obvious.[7] It must be an advancement beyond the prior art, which is generally defined as the knowledge available at a given time to a person of ordinary skill in the art. If it is not, the invention is not entitled to patent protection and an infringement claim will fail. The determination of whether a patent is obvious, and thus not protected, is one of the most commonly litigated issues in patent law.

A patent infringement claim may be formulated as a "literal" infringement or as an "equivalent" infringement. When the patented invention is a device, the plaintiff-patentee must establish that the infringer "makes, uses, or sells" a device that includes each of the elements identified in the patent claim. Proving a literal infringement is often difficult when minor variations to the invention have been made by the alleged infringer. Thus, it should not be surprising that clever infringers often attempt this ploy to avoid literal infringement claims.

When it is not possible to prove a literal claim, the patentee still may be entitled to protection. If the infringing product appropriates the essence of the patented invention, the doctrine of equivalents may apply to give the patentee protection from infringement. The doctrine is intended to prevent fraud on the patent by an unscrupulous copyist.

---

6. 35 U.S.C. § 102 (2006).
7. 35 U.S.C. § 103 (2006). In *Graham v. John Deere Co.*, 383 U.S. 1 (1966), the U.S. Supreme Court sets out the contemporary methodology for ascertaining non-obviousness.

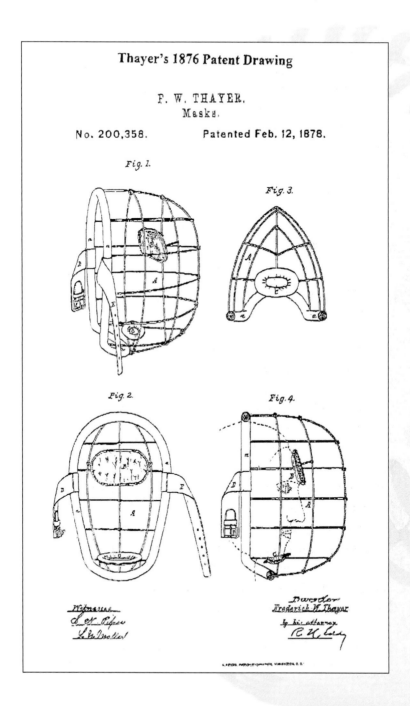

Thayer's 1876 Patent Drawing

F. W. THAYER.
Masks.

No. 200,358.   Patented Feb. 12, 1878.

Fig. 1.

Fig. 3.

Fig. 2.

Fig. 4.

Thayer's Legal Complaint

Thayer charged the defendants with infringing his patent. The purpose and description stated in the patent are:

> It is intended to protect the face of a player from being hit or injured by a baseball while in flight towards him, and also, at the same time, to not materially obstruct his sight. It is usually to be worn by the catcher, or person in rear of the striker or bat wielder. It consists of a forehead and chin rest, or bottom bearing, and a wire cage to receive them, and extend about the face, * * * and provided with straps, or means of securing the cage to the head of the player.

The Spalding brothers offered a variety of defenses. First, they claimed that Thayer's patent was "limited to the rests supported by wires reaching from the pads to the wires of the frame." Their mask was different from Thayer's and, thus, did not constitute an infringement. Second, they argued that Thayer's mask "is nothing but the old fencing mask," and didn't meet the requirements for patentability. Therefore, the mask was not entitled to a patent in the first place. Finally, they argued that there had been "prior public use of the device for more than two years." To the extent that the safety mask had been in actual "prior public use" before Thayer received his patent, the defendants argued Thayer was not entitled to patent protection.

The court rejected the defendants' arguments. It found that the defendants "make and sell a face mask formed of a wire cage and frame, in the same manner as the complainant's," and that their "head and chin rests perform the same function as that performed by the same elements in the patent, and no other." Therefore, the defendants' mask was treated as an equivalent of Thayer's mask.

As previously noted, the legal doctrine of equivalents operates to prevent the infringer from avoiding an infringement claim by adopting minor changes or substitutions to the protected invention. When the accused product performs substantially the same overall function, in the same way, to obtain the same result as the claimed invention, the doctrine of equivalents allows the patentee to successfully pursue the infringement claim. The court used this analysis to find the defendants' mask an equivalent.

The court also rejected defendants' claim that the claimed invention was simply "an old fencing mask." First, the court noted that the Thayer patent contained a disclaimer: "I do not claim a 'fencing-mask' as usually made of woven wire." Second, the court found patentable differences between the use and the construction of the two masks. The fencing mask required neither a head-rest nor chin-rest. On the other hand, these were important components of the baseball mask. The first claim of the patent is for the combination of the face-guard and the forehead and chin rests. The second claim is for the open cage provided with a forehead-rest. The fencing mask did not show these rests in any form. While the fencing mask and baseball mask were analogous in their use, the court found "enough difference between them to make that difference patentable."

The defendants' final argument, prior use, also failed. Albert G. Spalding and another witness testified that the baseball mask was used during a game played in Boston in the fall of 1875. The court was not persuaded. It found that the testimony did not "establish such prior use by strong and convincing proof." The testimony was insufficient to support the defendants' burden of proof.

As a result, the court found that Thayer's patent was valid, that the defendants infringed it, and that Thayer was entitled to damages. But that was not the end of the story.

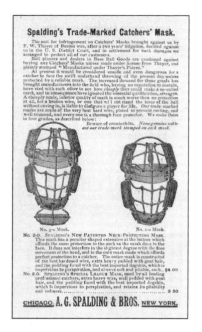

The Spaldings were sharp businessmen, and were not about to let their litigation loss to Thayer interfere with the advancement of their business. A Spalding advertisement touting the "Spalding's Trade-Marked Catchers' Mask" shortly appeared after they lost the case:

The suit for infringement on Catchers' Masks brought against us by F.W. Thayer [which confirms the misspelling of Spalding in the case caption and references in the court's opinion] of Boston was, after two years' litigation, decided against us in the U.S. District Court, and in settlement for back damages we arranged to protect all our customers.

Ball players and dealers in Base Ball Goods are cautioned against buying any Catchers' Masks unless made under a license from Thayer, and plainly stamped 'Manufactured under Thayer's Patent.'

At present it would be considered unsafe and even dangerous for a catcher to face the swift underhand throwing of the present day unless protected by a reliable mask. . . Our trade-marked masks are made of the very best hard wire, plated to prevent rusting, and well trimmed, and everyone is a thorough face protector.

In short, if you can't beat them, join them. The ad encourages folks to buy Spalding catcher masks and to watch out for evil counterfeiters.

A.G. Spalding left several footprints or spike marks on the game of baseball. As a team owner of the White Stockings from 1882 to 1891, Spalding was a strong advocate of the "reserve clause," which is subsequently explored in the case of *Flood v. Kuhn* in chapter 5. He also led the National League's effort to crush the Player's League, which had been established by the first ballplayers' union.

As fans and players know, the Spalding name is stamped on today's baseballs, gloves, and even catcher's masks. Their success is a Darwinian tribute to adaptability.

Umpire's Ruling

The Cost of Protection

While the modern fan cannot imagine a catcher squatting behind home plate without protection, it comes at a cost. Occasionally, a pitch gets stuck in the catcher's mask or between the chest protector and the uniform shirt. When a pitch "lodges in the umpire's or catcher's mask or paraphernalia, and remains out of play," the ball is dead and runners advance one base without risk of being put out.[1]

This rule does not apply when a foul tip lodges in the catcher's mask, as a foul tip is in play only when it is caught in the catcher's glove; otherwise, it is a dead ball. A foul tip on the third strike constitutes a strike out only if it is caught, and the catch cannot be on the rebound unless it has first hit the catcher's glove or hand.[2]

Once upon a time, the game was played without fielding gloves. That time has long passed, and the rules address permissible glove characteristics. Different limitations apply for gloves worn by catchers, first basemen, pitchers, and other defensive players.[3] One rule applies to all gloves—a glove can be used to stop a ball only while the glove is worn by the fielder. If a fielder throws a glove at and hits a fair ball, the batter automatically gets three bases and any base runner scores; the batter may also try to score but can be put out. If the umpire believes the ball would have cleared the fence on the fly but for the deflection, the hit is ruled a home run.[4] If the fielder throws a glove at and hits a thrown ball, the penalty is two bases.[5]

---

1. Rule 5.09(g).
2. Rule 2.00 (foul tip).
3. Rules 1.14–15.
4. Rule 7.05(c).
5. Rule 7.05(e).

MLB's Historical Antitrust Exemption

Federal Baseball Club of Baltimore v. National League, 259 U.S. 200 (1922)[1]

Any business that operates in interstate commerce is subject to the federal antitrust laws.

Federal Baseball was the first case challenging baseball under the federal antitrust laws. Baseball fans will recognize the facts as an early variation of the "squeeze play."[2]

The federal Sherman Antitrust Act, which was enacted by Congress in 1890, provides that "every contract, combination in the form of trust or otherwise, or conspiracy, in restraint of trade or commerce among the several States, or with foreign nations, is declared to be illegal." It also states that "every person who shall monopolize, or attempt to monopolize, or combine or conspire with any other person or persons, to monopolize any part of the trade or commerce among the several States, or with foreign nations, shall be deemed guilty of a felony. . . ." If a business

---

1. *Available at* http://www.supreme.justia.com/us/259/200/case.html (last visited Sept. 28, 2008.)

2. The squeeze play in baseball consists of a sacrifice bunt with a runner on third and fewer than two outs. The batter bunts and is willing to be thrown out at first base as long as the runner on third scores.

is not engaged in interstate commerce, the Sherman Act does not apply.

In 1903, the National and American Leagues signed a National Agreement.[3] In 1913, a new "major" Federal League was created by a group of wealthy businessmen from an existing "minor" league. The upstart new league erected eight new ball parks and touched off a bidding war for the most promising "star" players.

In 1915, a "peace agreement" with major league baseball (MLB) terminated the Federal League through a "squeeze play" when the National and American Leagues assumed its debts and acquired its most profitable assets. The defendants also agreed to pay the other Federal League owners to dissolve the league. There was another significant incentive. Some of the Federal League members were allowed to purchase franchises in the American or National Leagues. But Baltimore was not. It was squeezed out.

The Federal Baseball Club of Baltimore didn't like it. As a result, Baltimore club owners brought suit against the National and American Leagues and others for conspiring to monopolize

---

3. The preamble to the agreement provides:

This Agreement, made and entered into by and between the National League and American Association of Professional Base Ball Clubs, and the American League of Professional Base Ball Clubs, known and designated herein as Major Leagues, parties of the first part, each with the other and both, jointly and severally, by and with the National Association of Professional Base Ball Leagues, known and referred to herein as Minor Leagues, party of the second part, shall be styled the National Agreement, and shall have for its objects:

(1) Perpetuation of base ball as the national pastime of America, by surrounding it with such safeguards as will warrant absolute public confidence in its integrity and methods, and by maintaining a high standard of skill and sportsmanship in its players.

(2) Protection of the property rights of those engaged in base ball as a business without sacrificing the spirit of competition in the conduct of the clubs.

(3) Promotion of the welfare of ball players as a class by developing and perfecting them in their profession and enabling them to secure adequate compensation for expertness.

(4) Adoption of a uniform code of rules for playing base ball.

the business of baseball in violation of the Sherman Antitrust Act. Baltimore argued that the court must decide "whether organized baseball is above the law, or the law is above them." To add some zip to its pitch, Baltimore claimed that baseball magnates were "highwaymen" and professional ballplayers little more than "chattels and slaves" because of the reserve clause that allowed them to be "bought and sold." The leagues thundered back that the "world's championship series" would have to be done away with should the National Agreement be held unlawful.

Baltimore obtained a verdict in the trial court in the amount of $80,000, and a judgment for treble that amount was entered for violating the act. The Court of Appeals reversed on the theory that the Sherman Antitrust Act did not apply. Baltimore took the case to the U.S. Supreme Court, where it whiffed.

Baltimore's principal complaint was that the defendants destroyed the Federal League by buying up the other clubs and in one way or another inducing them, except for it, to leave the Federal League. Without other league teams to compete against, Baltimore was left out in the cold.

In short, these actions, according to Baltimore, violated the Sherman Act. Because the antitrust law requires "commerce among the several States," Baltimore argued that the defendants were engaged in interstate commerce by traveling across state lines and, thus, the business of baseball was subject to the law. Baseball as a business, Baltimore argued, was distinguishable from merely playing the game as a sport for physical exercise and diversion. There is a difference between little league and the majors.

The historical antitrust exemption for baseball is traceable to the *Federal Baseball* decision. The case continues to influence the debate on the continuance of the exemption. MLB's control over the relocation of teams is one reason the exemption continues to be important. In addition, baseball engages in other anti-competitive activities that are possible only because of the exemption.

The following are excerpts from the landmark opinion by Justice Oliver Wendell Holmes. The references to the word "business" are italicized for emphasis:

> It is alleged that these defendants conspired to monopolize the base ball *business*, the means adopted being set forth with a detail which, in the view that we take, it is unnecessary to repeat. . . .
>
> The decision of the Court of Appeals went to the root of the case and if correct makes it unnecessary to consider other serious difficulties in the way of the plaintiff's recovery. A summary statement of the nature of the *business* involved will be enough to present the point. The clubs composing the Leagues are in different cities and for the most part in different States. The end of the elaborate organizations and sub-organizations that are described in the pleadings and evidence is that these clubs shall play against one another in public exhibitions for money, one or the other club crossing a state line in order to make the meeting possible. When as the result of these contests one club has won the pennant of its League and another club has won the pennant of the other League, there is a final competition for the world's championship between these two. Of course the scheme requires constantly repeated travelling on the part of the clubs, which is provided for, controlled and disciplined by the organizations, and this it is said means commerce among the States. But we are of opinion that the Court of Appeals was right.

The *business* is giving exhibitions of base ball, which are purely state affairs. It is true that in order to attain for these exhibitions the great popularity that they have achieved, competitions must be arranged between clubs from different cities and States. But the fact that in order to give the exhibitions the Leagues must induce free persons to cross state lines and must arrange and pay for their doing so is not enough to change the character of the *business*. According to the distinction insisted upon in *Hooper v. California, 155 U. S. 648, 655*, the transport is a mere incident, not the essential thing. That to which it is incident, the exhibition, although made for money would not be called trade of commerce in the commonly accepted use of those words. As it is put by defendant, personal effort, not related to production, is not a subject of commerce. That which in its consummation is not commerce does not become commerce among the States because the transportation that we have mentioned takes place. To repeat the illustrations given by the Court below, a firm of lawyers sending out a member to argue a case, or the Chautauqua lecture bureau sending out lecturers, does not engage in such commerce because the lawyer or lecturer goes to another State.

If we are right the plaintiff's *business* is to be described in the same way and the restrictions by contract that prevented the plaintiff from getting players to break their bargains and the other conduct charged against the defendants were not an interference with commerce among the States.

Judgment affirmed.

43

In short, the Supreme Court reasoned that baseball was purely a state affair. It was not interstate commerce and, therefore, not subject to the Sherman Antitrust Act. Holmes reasoned that giving baseball exhibitions for profit was not "trade or commerce in the commonly accepted use of those words" because "personal effort, not related to production, is not a subject of commerce."

The court did not explain the basis for distinguishing "trade or commerce" related to the production of industrial products from those involving "personal effort," such as services. The language of the Sherman Act does not draw such distinction. The court also concluded that baseball was not deemed interstate because the movement of ball clubs across state lines was merely "incidental" to the business. At the time, the business of National and American Leagues was local.

Fifty years after *Federal Baseball*, Supreme Court Justice William O. Douglas referred to the decision as "a derelict in the stream of the law that we, its creator, should remove." Others have called the decision the metaphorical equivalent of a "wild pitch." With the passage of time, there is much to be said for this criticism. In the field of sports, the baseball decision is an anomaly. The Supreme Court has held other professional sports, such as boxing, football, and basketball, subject to the Sherman Antitrust Act. Thus, it is reasonable to ask: Why not baseball?

A couple of points are worth considering. First, the historical context of *Federal Baseball* is the early 1900s. The interstate commercialization of the game through radio, television, and podcasts on the Internet had not yet occurred. There also was no revenue sharing. Thus, the business side of the game had not evolved to what it is today.

Second, the court's analysis focused on whether the interstate aspects were essential to its character or merely "incidental" to the business. The court says, "the business is giving exhibitions of baseball, which are purely state affairs." While arguably this may have rung with some veracity at the time, surely it is no longer true. Baseball is big business. Significant interstate rivalries exist today. The interstate transport of players and equipment as "a mere incident" to the business is a quaint view of today's reality.

The view that baseball should never be deemed interstate commerce is a crabbed view of what the court actually said in *Federal Baseball*. Subsequent developments have transformed the "essential thing" into an interstate transaction. The antitrust exemption for baseball is apt to be treated at some point as a historical curiosity.

Justice Holmes, were he alive today, might not object. Holmes persuasively argued in his classic article, "The Path of the Law," the dynamic nature of the law: "[i]t is revolting to have no better reason for a rule of law than that so it was laid down in the time of Henry IV [or 1922]. It is still more revolting if the grounds upon which it was laid down have vanished long since, and the rule simply persists from blind imitation of the past."[4] Times change and so should the law.

The real question is who should change it, the Supreme Court or Congress?

---

4. O.W. Holmes, *The Path of the Law*, 10 HARV. L. REV. 457, 469 (1897).

Umpire's Ruling

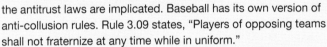

Collusion on the Field

When supposed business competitors—such as baseball owners—collude with each other, the antitrust laws are implicated. Baseball has its own version of anti-collusion rules. Rule 3.09 states, "Players of opposing teams shall not fraternize at any time while in uniform."

You don't need a big-screen TV to see that this rule is low on the list for enforcement. Nothing is more common than to see a first baseman conferring with an opponent who has just reached base. First baseman Sean Casey is so well known for this activity that he is nicknamed "The Mayor."

This rule was taken more seriously in the not-distant past. As recently as the early 1990s, one member of the umpiring crew would arrive at the field early enough to observe batting practice and take note of opposing players who spent too much time talking with each other.[1]

---

1. Joe Frisaro, *Girardi's reported conversation with Lieber sparks debate*, http://mlb.mlb.com/news/arti.cle.jsp?ymd=20070228&content_id=1819906&vkey=news_mlb&fext=.jsp&c_id=mlb.

The Supreme Court "Balks" at Changing the Antitrust Exemption

Flood v. Kuhn et al., 407 U.S. 258 (1972)[1]

The antitrust laws of the United States, and the Sherman Act in particular, are the Magna Carta of the nation's free enterprise system. In 1972, the application of the antitrust laws to baseball's reserve system was once again before the Supreme Court in *Flood v. Kuhn*. Under the reserve system in effect at the time, a player was tied to a ball club under a perpetual series of one-year options. The Supreme Court refused to untangle this thorny problem saying that it was Congress's job.

The Facts

In the late 1950s and 1960s, Curt Flood was a well-known major league baseball (MLB) player. He rose to fame with the St. Louis Cardinals from 1958 to 1969. During his playing career, he received many kudos, including seven Golden Glove Awards. As

---

1. *Available at* http://supreme.justia.com/us/407/258/case.html (last visited Sept. 28, 2008).

the title to this inning reveals, he also occupies a special place in the record book of the Supreme Court.

In 1969, Flood was traded by the Cardinals to the Philadelphia Phillies in a multi-player transaction. Notice of his involuntary reassignment occurred after he was traded. Flood complained to Bowie Kuhn, the commissioner of baseball, and asked to be made a free agent in order to be able to bargain with any other major league team. Kuhn denied Flood's request based on the "reserve clause," which was part of the standard player's contract at the time.[2]

Flood argued that the reserve system effectively made him the "property" of the Cardinals and unfairly constrained his personal freedom. In 1970, Flood acted. He filed an antitrust suit against the commissioner, the presidents of the American and National Leagues, and the 24 major league clubs in the federal court for the Southern District of New York. He charged the defendants with violating the federal antitrust laws, as well as federal civil rights statutes, state statutes, and the common law, as well as with the involuntary servitude provisions of the Thirteenth Amendment.

2. Flood refused to play for Philadelphia in 1970, and he sat out the season. At the end of the season, Philadelphia sold its rights to Flood to the Washington Senators. He started the 1971 season with Washington, but left the club and baseball in April.

The courts were not writing on a blank slate. In 1922, the Supreme Court had rejected the claim that the antitrust laws applied to baseball in *Federal Baseball*, as seen in the preceding inning. Moreover, the standard "reserve clause" had been before the Supreme Court in 1953 in *Toolson v. New York Yankees.*[3] The challenge to the reserve clause in *Toolson* was rejected based on its earlier decision in *Federal Baseball*. The court affirmed the principle that the business of providing public baseball games for profit between clubs of professional baseball players was not within the scope of the federal antitrust laws.

As expected, Flood lost his antitrust claim in the trial court based on *Federal Baseball* and *Toolson*. Flood's other theories also were rejected. Flood appealed to the Second Circuit, which tepidly felt "compelled to affirm" the district court.

The Supreme Court granted certiorari to look "at this troublesome and unusual situation." Unless the Supreme Court was willing to change its mind, Flood was going to lose in much the same way John Henry, the "steel driving man," lost his struggle against the odds.[4]

---

3. Toolson v. New York Yankees, Inc., 346 U.S. 356 (1953).

4. The earliest "John Henry" ballads originated in the oral tradition of hammer songs in the 1870s and evolved over time. This is one version of the lyrics:

When John Henry was a little baby
He was sitting on his momma's knee
Reached out his hand picked up a little piece of steel
Said this is gonna be the death of me . . .

John Henry said to his Captain
A man ain't nothin' but a man
And before I let that steam drill beat me down
I will die with this hammer in my hand . . .

They took John Henry to the graveyard
laid him down in the sand
Every locomotive comin' a-rolling by by by
hollered "there lies a steel-drivin' man man man
there lies a steel-drivin' man!

The Reserve System

From 1887 through its restructuring in 1976, a player was bound to a team for life through "the reserve clause."[5] A baseball team could renew a player's contract for one year or for as long as the team wanted to keep the player. The "free agency" movement gained traction with Flood's challenge to the reserve system.[6]

The reserve system centered on the uniformity of player contracts; the confinement of the player to the club that has him under the contract; the assignability of the player's contract; and the ability of the club annually to renew the contract unilaterally, subject to a stated salary minimum.

At the time *Flood* was litigated, the reserve system provided:

A. Rule 3 of the Major League Rules provided in part:

(a) UNIFORM CONTRACT. To preserve morale and to produce the similarity of conditions necessary to keen competition, the contracts between all clubs and their players in the Major Leagues shall be in a single form which shall be prescribed by the Major League Executive Council. No club shall make a contract different from the uniform contract or a contract containing a non-reserve clause, except with the written approval of the Commissioner. . . .

(g) TAMPERING. To preserve discipline and compe-

---

5. The players' union succeeded in partially unraveling the reserve system through arbitration in 1976, but the baseball owners still use their monopoly to control such matters as franchise location, league competition, and broadcast rights.

6. After the Supreme Court decided *Flood*, an arbitration system for the players' union and owner disputes was put into effect. In 1975, pitchers Andy Messersmith and Dave McNally played without contracts, arguing that their contracts could not be renewed if they were never signed. An arbitrator agreed, and they became the first free agents. In the 1976 collective bargaining agreement, the players' union and the owners agreed to a restructuring of the reserve system.

In 1989, an arbitrator found that 26 MLB owners conspired to kill the free agency agreement after the 1985 season.

tition, and to prevent the enticement of players, coaches, managers and umpires, there shall be no negotiations or dealings respecting employment, either present or prospective, between any player, coach or manager and any club other than the club with which he is under contract or acceptance of terms, or by which he is reserved, or which has the player on its Negotiation List, or between any umpire and any league other than the league with which he is under contract or acceptance of terms, unless the club or league with which he is connected shall have, in writing, expressly authorized such negotiations or dealings prior to their commencement.

B. Rule 9 of the Major League Rules provided in part:

(a) NOTICE. A club may assign to another club an existing contract with a player. The player, upon receipt of written notice of such assignment, is by his contract bound to serve the assignee. After the date of such assignment all rights and obligations of the assignor clubs thereunder shall become the rights and obligations of the assignee club . . . .

C. Rules 3 and 9 of the Professional Baseball Rules contain provisions parallel to those just quoted.

D. The Uniform Player's Contract provided in part:

4. (a) . . . The Player agrees that, in addition to other remedies, the Club shall be entitled to injunctive and other equitable relief to prevent a breach of this contract by the Player, including, among others, the right to enjoin the Player from playing baseball for any other person or organization during the term of this contract.

5. (a). The Player agrees that, while under contract,

and prior to expiration of the Club's right to renew this contract, he will not play baseball otherwise than for the Club, except that the Player may participate in post-season games under the conditions prescribed in the Major League Rules. . . .

6. (a) The Player agrees that this contract may be assigned by the Club (and reassigned by any assignee Club) to any other Club in accordance with the Major League Rules and the Professional Baseball Rules.

10. (a) On or before January 15 (or if a Sunday, then the next preceding business day) of the year next following the last playing season covered by this contract, the Club may tender to the Player a contract for the term of that year by mailing the same to the Player at his address following his signature hereto, or if none be given, then at his last address of record with the Club. If prior to the March 1 next succeeding said January 15, the Player and the Club have not agreed upon the terms of such contract, then on or before 10 days after said March 1, the Club shall have the right by written notice to the Player at said address to renew this contract for the period of one year on the same terms, except that the amount payable to the Player shall be such as the club shall fix in said notice; provided, however, that said amount, if fixed by a Major League Club, shall be an amount payable at a rate not less than 80% of the rate stipulated for the preceding year.

(b) The Club's right to renew this contract, as provided in subparagraph (a) of this paragraph 10, and the promise of the Player not to play otherwise than with the Club have been taken into consideration in determining the amount payable under paragraph 2 hereof.

The Supreme Court's Reprise

The Supreme Court balked at changing the law. The Court recognized that baseball was a business engaged in interstate commerce and that *Federal Baseball* was an aberration. Nevertheless, it reasoned that the aberration had been in place for a half a century. Therefore, its earlier decisions were entitled to the benefit of precedent, which lawyers call *stare decisis*.[7]

The Court reasoned that Congress, which wrote the antitrust laws, had not acted to bring baseball's reserve system within the reach of the antitrust statutes. This inaction, the Court concluded, was "something other than mere congressional silence and passivity." It was positive inaction.

The Court also expressed concern about the confusion and the retroactivity problems that inevitably would result with a judicial overturning of *Federal Baseball*. If change is to be made, it should come by legislative action that, by its nature, is only prospective in operation. In short, Congress was at the plate, not the Court.

Congress Steps to the Plate

Congress partially accepted the Court's invitation to act. In 1998, it passed the Curt Flood Act.[8] As evidenced by the stated purpose of the law, the act is limited to MLB labor matters:

> It is the purpose of this legislation to state that major
> league baseball players are covered under the antitrust
> laws (i.e., that major league baseball players will have

---

7. The central idea of *stare decisis* is consistency. A subsequent judicial decision should follow both the reasoning and the result of a prior decision. The Supreme Court may refuse, however, to follow an earlier decision when it finds that that decision is based on an unsound principle.

8. 15 U.S.C. § 26 (b). Curt Flood Act of 1998, Pub. L. No. 105-297, 112 Stat. 2824 (1998).

the same rights under the antitrust laws as do other professional athletes, e.g., football and basketball players), along with a provision that makes it clear that the passage of this Act does not change the application of the antitrust laws in any other context or with respect to any other person or entity.

Subsection (b) now expressly provides that "the conduct, acts, practices, or agreements of persons in the business of organized professional major league baseball directly relating to or affecting *employment* of major league baseball players to play baseball at the major league level are subject to the antitrust laws to the same extent such conduct, acts, practices, or agreements would be subject to the antitrust laws if engaged in by persons in any other professional sports business affecting interstate commerce."

It also states:

No court shall rely on this section as a basis for changing the application of the antitrust laws to any conduct, acts, practices, or agreements other than in subsection (a). This section does not create, permit or imply a cause of action by which to challenge under the antitrust laws, or otherwise apply the antitrust laws to, any conduct, acts, practices, or agreements that do not directly relate to or affect employment of major league baseball players to play baseball at the major league level. . . .

Several aspects of the Curt Flood Act are notable. First, the traditional antitrust exemption is continued. Second, the change applies to "major league baseball players" in their employment relationship. Without the continued antitrust exemption, the minor league "farm system" would be subject to challenge.

Flood's Legacy

Although Curt Flood did not end the reserve system, he was a catalyst to changing it. At the memorial service for Flood in 1997, Marvin Miller, the former executive director of the Major League Baseball Players Association, honored him with these words:

> At the time Curt Flood decided to challenge baseball's reserve clause, he was perhaps the sport's premier centerfielder. And yet he chose to fight an injustice, knowing that even if by some miracle he won, his career as a professional player would be over. At no time did he waver in his commitment and determination. He had experienced something that was inherently unfair and was determined to right the wrong, not so much for himself, but for those who would come after him. Few praised him for this, then or now. There is no Hall of Fame for people like Curt.
>
> As Curt Flood realized, the fight for justice is never ending.

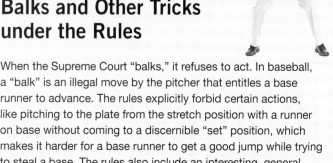

Umpire's Ruling

Balks and Other Tricks under the Rules

When the Supreme Court "balks," it refuses to act. In baseball, a "balk" is an illegal move by the pitcher that entitles a base runner to advance. The rules explicitly forbid certain actions, like pitching to the plate from the stretch position with a runner on base without coming to a discernible "set" position, which makes it harder for a base runner to get a good jump while trying to steal a base. The rules also include an interesting, general comment: "Umpires should bear in mind that the purpose of the balk rule is to prevent the pitcher from deliberately deceiving the base runner. If there is doubt in the umpire's mind, the 'intent' of the pitcher should govern."[1]

But the rules do not consistently preclude trickery. Indeed, every pitch is an effort to trick the batter—the pitcher need not warn the batter that a change up is on the way, for example. The explanation cannot be that tricking the hitter is fine but tricking the runner is not. The pitcher is precluded by the balk rule from faking a throw to first while in contact with the pitching rubber,[2] but may fake a throw to second or third, and those fakes are a form of trickery too. The pitcher can even fake a throw to first as long as contact with the rubber is broken first.

Other rules do seem aimed to protect against trickery. For example, with runners on first and second or with the bases loaded, the infield-fly rule dictates that a pop fly that should be caught with reasonable effort by an infielder (even if the infielder would need to go into the outfield to catch it) is an automatic out when there are fewer than two outs in the inning. Otherwise, a fielder would be able to trick the runner by letting the ball drop and getting a double play by throwing out two of the base runners who, without the rule, would be forced to attempt to advance. While the infield-fly rule does not apply to a line drive (or to fly balls in some situations), a separate rule has a similar effect when a fielder intentionally drops a line drive or fly ball.[3]

But here too, not all tricks are precluded. The rule on dropping a line drive does not apply if a fielder just lets the liner fall without touching it first, even though that act would certainly trick the runner too.

One play even has the word "trick" in its name—the "hidden-ball trick." But the trick is more difficult to pull off than many believe. In the 1993 movie *Rookie of the Year*, the rookie—a 12-year-old who gained the ability to throw more than 90 m.p.h. after an arm injury but lost the ability near the end of the movie—and his first baseman pull the trick after a meeting at the mound. While the base runner thinks the pitcher is holding the ball, he has actually given it to the first baseman, who tags the runner out. But it appears that the trick was not a legal one in the movie. (And if we're criticizing the movie for its lack of realism, we might also note that it features the Cubs' winning the World Series.) The pitcher appears to be standing "on or astride" the pitching rubber during the play, which is a balk if the pitcher does not have the ball.[4] Even if the pitcher is not in that position (and it is a little hard to be clear from the VHS of the movie), the play occurs immediately after the pitcher meets with his entire infield at the mound. Presumably, time was out during this meeting; otherwise, the runner would have advanced during the conference. But the ball would need to be put in play for the runner to be put out, as a player cannot be put out while the ball is dead.[5] And the umpire can declare the ball in play only when the pitcher is on the rubber holding the ball,[6] which cannot occur if the first baseman has the ball. This rule is an obstacle to any attempt to pull the hidden-ball play after time has been called for a conference.

In summary, trickery is forbidden by the rules except when it isn't. And movies aren't real.

---

1. Rule 8.05 Comment.
2. Rule 8.05(b).
3. Rule 6.05(l).
4. Rule 8.05(i).
5. Rule 5.02.
6. Rule 5.11.

"Hey, Beerman!"

Donchez v. Coors Brewing Co.,
392 F.3d 1211 (10th Cir. 2004)[1]

obert Donchez was headed for fame. He earned an MBA from Fordham University, and worked as a financial accountant and analyst on Wall Street before heading to Denver, Colorado. In early 1993, he decided to use his marketing talents by becoming a beer vendor for the Colorado Rockies baseball team. The Rockies hired him and gave him the badge number "0001," which identified him as the first licensed beer vendor in the Rockies' history. He had taken an important step on the ladder to success.

As a beer vendor, Robert created the marketing character "Bob the Beerman." He became known for entertaining the crowd with his antics during the games, as well as making ample quantities of beer available to thirsty fans. His sales pitch for beer included such crowd pleasers as "My favorite word in the English language: Beer! Two favorite words: Cold Beer! Three favorite words: Cold Beer Man!" He was a hit.

In 1993, Robert registered "Bob the Beerman" for service

---

1. *Available at* http://www.ca10.uscourts.gov/opinions/03/03-1462.pdf (last visited Sept. 28, 2008).

mark protection under Colorado law. He was on a roll. In 1994, he wrote a book about his Beerman experiences during the first season at the Rockies' baseball games. In 1996, he approached Coors armed with his book, a video, and the idea of using "Bob the Beerman" in the Coors advertising campaign. His beer pitch fell as flat as day-old-beer, and he was unsuccessful in closing the deal.

The following year, Coors started a national television advertising campaign for its Coors Light beer using various actors and an actress portraying beer vendors playfully bantering with the crowd. The advertisements used the vendors "interacting with the crowd in amusing ways at sporting events." "Some of the vendors call[ed] themselves or [we]re referred to by customers as 'beerman,' or 'the beerman,' or 'Hey, beerman,' or 'Hey, beerstud.'"

Robert believed he had been ripped off by their advertisements. He sued Coors and FCB, the company that produced the advertisements, in the U.S. District Court for the District of Colorado. He threw an eight-pack of legal claims at the defendants. He sued for violation of service mark infringement under Colorado law, common law service mark infringement, unfair competition in violation of the federal Lanham Act, violation of the common law right of publicity, violation of the Colorado Consumer Protection Act, unjust enrichment, and unfair misappropriation and exploitation of business value. How could he lose?

The district court granted summary judgment for the defendants on all counts. Robert demanded another round at the bar of justice by taking his case to the Tenth Circuit Court of Appeals. The appellate court affirmed the district court. Among other things, it found that the term "beerman" was not protected and that the Coors advertising campaign did not violate his "right of publicity." The Tenth Circuit presumably quenched his thirst for further litigation.

Service Marks

A service mark identifies a service, whereas a trademark identifies a good or product. Both types of intellectual property serve the common purpose of allowing a consumer to reliably identify the source of the service or the good or product. The unauthorized use of a service mark that is likely to cause consumer confusion infringes the service mark and is actionable.

Section 1127 of the Lanham Act provides:

> The term "service mark" means any word, name, symbol, or device, or any combination thereof—(1) used by a person, or (2) which a person has a bona fide intention to use in commerce and applies to register on the principal register established by this chapter, to identify and distinguish the services of one person, including a unique service, from the services of others and to indicate the source of the services, even if that source is unknown. Titles, character names, and other distinctive features of radio or television programs may be registered as service marks notwithstanding that they, or the programs, may advertise the goods of the sponsor.

A typical service mark would include, for example, Google or Federal Express.

Robert's first three claims depended on proving that his "service mark rights" were in fact protected by the law. To qualify for protection, the service mark must be distinctive—it must identify and distinguish the service. In addition to proving his "beerman" rights were protected, he would also have to demonstrate that the defendants' use of a similar or identical mark would cause consumer confusion.

A "generic" service mark, which is essentially a common

description of services, is not protected by the law because it does not distinguish the service. Granting rights for a generic term would, in itself, cause considerable consumer confusion.

Robert argued that "beerman" was not a generic mark. Rather, it was a descriptive mark, which he maintained is protectable. A descriptive mark may be protected when the service mark has acquired a secondary meaning in the minds of the public. Robert argued that the "beerman" portion of the mark was descriptive because most members of the public, he argued, would associate the mark with his services.

The appellate court reasoned, however, that the "beerman" portion of the "Bob the Beerman" service mark was generic. It was simply the general combination of two words, "beer" and "man."

Robert's descriptive-secondary meaning argument fell as flat as two-day-old beer. A "descriptive mark" claim requires supporting evidence, usually based on consumer surveys or testimony from consumers. The court found that Robert had failed to provide sufficient evidence to establish that the public, whether viewed locally, regionally, or nationally, would associate the term "beerman" with his character. In short, it had not acquired a "secondary meaning."

Therefore, a rational jury lacked sufficient facts to support his argument, so the defendants were entitled to a judgment as a matter of law. The court put it this way: "We conclude that Donchez has failed to present sufficient evidence to allow a jury to find he has a protectable interest in the mark 'beerman.'"

Right of Publicity

Most states have adopted the right of publicity by statute or case law. The historical foothold to the modern right of publicity is the right of privacy. In 1902, the New York Court of Appeals[2] rejected the claim for emotional distress resulting from the unauthorized use of the plaintiff's photograph in a commercial advertisement. Arguably, this use infringed the plaintiff's right of privacy. To correct this shortcoming in the law, the New York legislature responded by enacting a statute that imposed liability for unauthorized use of a person's name, portrait, or picture for "advertising purposes or for the purposes of trade." The right was now recognized.

Although originally based on a person's right of privacy, today the law is recognized as a type of intellectual property right that gives a person the exclusive right to commercially exploit one's identity. Using another person's identity, such as that person's name or likeness, without consent, for commercial purposes may constitute a violation of the right of publicity.

Various rationales support its recognition. The right can be

---

2. Roberson v. Rochester Folding Box Co., 64 N.E. 442 (N.Y. 1902).

justified on the ground that it prevents free-riding on another's identity. It is inequitable to pirate another's labor and then either "palm off" those fruits as one's own, which deceives the public, or gain an unearned commercial benefit by reaping where one has not sown.

The Restatement (Third) of Unfair Competition, Section 46, states the following on the right of publicity: "One who appropriates the commercial value of a person's identity by using without consent the person's name, likeness, or other indicia of identity for purposes of trade is subject to liability." Comment (c) to this section contains the following explanation:

> Recognition of a right of publicity has been justified on numerous grounds. Like the right of privacy, the right of publicity protects an individual's interest in personal dignity and autonomy. With its emphasis on commercial interests, the right of publicity also secures for plaintiffs the commercial value of their fame and prevents the unjust enrichment of others seeking to appropriate that value for themselves. The right to prohibit unauthorized commercial exploitation of one's identity allows a person to prevent harmful or excessive commercial use that may dilute the value of the identity. Although proof of deception or confusion is not an element of liability under this Section, the right of publicity indirectly affords protection against false suggestions of endorsement or sponsorship. Some decisions also invoke an incentive rationale analogous to that supporting the recognition of exclusive rights under copyright and patent law.

Violation of the right of publicity gives rise to a cause of action under the umbrella of unfair competition. The Colorado

Supreme Court had not expressly recognized this type of tort, however, at the time Robert sued. Nevertheless, some lower Colorado courts had recognized the right of publicity, so it was an arguable theory.

Assuming that Colorado did in fact recognize the existence of the right of publicity, the Tenth Circuit still found that Robert struck out. It reasoned that he was required to prove that the defendants had used his "likeness" or "identity" to their commercial advantage. But there was no evidence that the defendants had done so. The Coors commercials bore no resemblance to him or his identity.

The argument that Coors had used the term "beerman" as well as certain characteristics similar to his character "Bob the Beerman" to its commercial advantage was therefore outside the protection of the law. The fact that Robert had registered his character with the Colorado authorities was ignored. Consequently, the Tenth Circuit found that the district court properly rejected Robert's right of publicity claim.

As a general proposition, the use of the identifying characteristics or attributes of a person may constitute the infringement of the right of publicity. In order to do so, however, the complained of infringing use must be so closely and uniquely linked to the individual that the use enables the defendant to appropriate the commercial value of the plaintiff's identity.

The general idea of using funny and colorful characters to sell beer is almost as old as beer itself. It has been around for a long time. The folks used in the Coors advertising campaign would not be mistaken for "Bob the Beerman." In the end, Robert was left standing without relief at the bar of justice.

Umpire's Ruling

Team Branding and Uniforms

"Beerman" may not conjure up the image of any particular beerman, but names like "Yankees," "Red Sox," and the like have more powerful branding effects, and the uniforms the teams wear assist in the process.

The Rules of Baseball require that players and coaches be "in uniform" if they are "on the field"; that rule does not apply to managers,[1] but all managers since the retirement of Connie Mack in the early 1950s have worn a uniform.[2] The uniform may not include a "pattern that imitates or suggests the shape of a baseball,"[3] presumably to prevent the design of a uniform that makes more difficult the batter's task of spotting the ball out of the pitcher's hand. Shiny attachments—in particular, "[g]lass buttons and polished metal"—are also specifically prohibited.[4]

Sartorial self expression is permitted by the rules governing the undershirt. While all players on a team must wear undershirts of the same color,[5] the rules specifically provide that "[s]leeve lengths may vary for individual players." However, to avoid anarchy, the rules also provide that for any given player, the sleeves must be "approximately the same length."[6]

While the uniform is important in branding the team, some other potential uses are forbidden. The cap cannot be used to catch or deflect a batted or thrown ball without incurring penalties like those incurred when a glove is thrown at a ball, discussed previously in Inning Three.

---

1. Rule 3.15.
2. http://www.en.wikipedia.org/wiki/Major_League_Baseball_uniforms.
3. Rule 1.11(e).
4. Rule 1.11(f).
5. Rule 1.11(a)(2).
6. Rule 1.11(c)(1).

Ballpark Legal Warfare

Padres L.P. v. Henderson, 114 Cal. App. 4th 495 (2003), *rehearing denied* (2004)[1]

T he chorus of "Take Me Out to the Ball Game" is traditionally sung during the seventh inning stretch.[2] For years, afficionados of the game have debated why the chorus is so popular. Harry Caray, whose rendition of the chorus enjoyed national popularity, once said, "I would always sing it, because I think it's the only song I knew the words to." Thus, perhaps the simplest explanation to its popularity is that the chorus is easy to sing.

Singing "Take Me Out to the Ball Game" at a new ballpark can be a memorable experience. In the last decade or so, 15 new

---

1. *Available at* http://www.precydent.com/htmlversion.html?id=87705 (last visited Sept. 28, 2008).

2. *"Take me out to the ball game,*
   Take me out with the crowd;
   Buy me some peanuts and Cracker Jack,
   I don't care if I never get back.
   Let me root, root, root for the home team,
   If they don't win, it's a shame.
   For it's one, two, three strikes, you're out,
   At the old ball game."

In 1908, Jack Norworth wrote the lyrics to "Take Me Out to the Ball Game." The lyrics were then set to music by Albert Von Tilzer. Although some of the lyrics were changed by Norworth in 1927, the above chorus remained the same.

major league baseball (MLB) ballparks have been built. The "House that Ruth Built," which was home of the New York Yankees from 1923 through 2008, was replaced with a new ball park due to open in 2009.

Building a new MLB ballpark is challenging. Locating a suitable new or replacement venue, arranging for the necessary financing, and overcoming land-use as well as associated environmental regulatory obstacles are hurdles that must be cleared. Convincing the public to support a MLB ballpark project, especially when public subsidies are involved, readily attracts naysayers.

Overcoming ballpark opposition is difficult even when a stadium project enjoys public support. Opponents to the project may file a series of lawsuits to defeat the project by delaying construction and increasing the cost of completion.

The story behind the completion of Petco Park, home of the National League (NL) San Diego Padres, illustrates the litigation challenges faced by the City of San Diego and Padres owner John Moores. The road to the completion of Petco was strewn with a series of lawsuits thrown at the Padres and the City of San Diego by J. Bruce Henderson, an attorney and former San Diego city councilman.

Before the first pitch was thrown at Petco, there were 17

lawsuits, a corruption probe,[3] and financing setbacks from the litigation. In the end, the lawsuits delayed the 2004 opening day by two seasons.[4] The additional cost from the delay ran in the millions of dollars.

Moores "slapped" back at Henderson. After it was reasonably apparent that Henderson was "out of legal challenges" to stop the Petco project, Moores filed suit against Henderson for the guerilla legal war he had waged against the project. Moores sued Henderson for the tort of malicious prosecution.

Although malicious prosecution claims are notoriously difficult to prove, the evidence was sufficient to establish a prima facie case of improper motive. The appellate court sent the case back to the superior court for further proceedings.

Pitching the Idea of a New Ballpark for the Padres

In the mid-1990s, Moores pitched the idea to city officials that the Padres needed their own ballpark in order "to remain competitive and to become financially stable." As a result, the city council established a task force to study the idea and, when the task force agreed that a new ballpark was needed, the city set up a second task force to recommend a site and to suggest various financing strategies. In January 1998, the second task force recommended siting the ballpark in downtown San Diego as part of a larger urban development project.

---

3. In 2000, a federal corruption investigation revealed that Councilwoman Valerie Stallings, during the same time the city council voted on the ballpark project, economically profited on the initial public offering of stock in a software company headed by Padres owner John Moores. Councilwoman Stallings pleaded guilty to two misdemeanors and subsequently resigned from office. Moores was cleared of any charges.

4. The Padres tasted sweet victory by beating the San Francisco Giants 4-3 in extra innings in front of 41,400 exuberant fans.

In August 1998, the city council enacted an election ordinance to place "Proposition C" on the November 1998 ballot.[5] The public would decide the basic merits of the ballpark. Petco was pitched to the public as part of a 26-block redevelopment, which included the ballpark as the "anchor." Proposition C authorized the city to enter into a memorandum of understanding (MOU) with the Padres, as well as other agencies, to move the ballpark redevelopment project forward with the public's blessing.

The idea that Proposition C was "more than just a ballpark" was seen by many voters as a significant advantage. But before the vote on Proposition C could take place, Henderson swung his litigation bat at Moores's pitch.

The Guerilla Legal Battle Starts

In his first lawsuit, *Mailhot I*, Henderson asked the Superior Court for declaratory and injunctive relief against the upcoming public vote on Proposition C on behalf of the named plaintiff, Jerry Mailhot. Henderson had a bag full of legal theories to support his position.

Henderson alleged that Proposition C, the MOU, and the ballot materials contained misleading statements. He also alleged that Proposition C violated the California Constitution "by conferring rights and imposing duties on a private entity." Henderson also maintained that Proposition C violated the California Constitution's and the San Diego City Charter's "one subject"

---

5. AUTHORIZING REDEVELOPMENT AND A BALLPARK. Shall an ordinance be adopted authorizing the City of San Diego to enter into agreements to redevelop an area of downtown, and construct a multiple use ballpark, provided that: 1) the City's participation requires no new taxes, is capped, and also limited to redevelopment funds and an amount equivalent to certain hotel tax revenue; and 2) the San Diego Padres guarantee substantial private contributions, pay all ballpark construction cost overruns, and play in San Diego until 2024?

rule, and that the vote was "premature" because the city had not prepared or certified an environmental impact report (EIR) for the project, as required by California environmental law.

But Henderson had not exhausted his legal arsenal in his first foray against the project. He asked the court to declare that San Diego's City Charter required a two-thirds' vote to pass Proposition C "because the City's financial obligations thereunder constituted a debt for the 1998-1999 fiscal year exceeding the City's available resources." You don't have to be a city attorney to realize that getting a two-thirds' vote for anything is difficult.

In September 1998, the superior court denied Henderson's petition in its entirety. Shortly thereafter, Henderson filed a notice of appeal challenging the court's denial. While the *Mailhot I* appeal was pending, the electorate approved Proposition C by a 60 to 40 percent margin on November 3, 1998. From Henderson's perspective, the fact that the public had endorsed the project by its vote was not the end of the matter.

Ignoring the result of the vote, Henderson next focused on financing and environmental considerations. The MOU specified that the city's contribution to the ballpark project would be capped at $225 million; the Padres would contribute $115 million and be responsible for any ballpark cost overruns. In early 1999, the city council passed an appropriation ordinance pursuant to the MOU that appropriated $225 million for the ballpark project. From this amount, the ordinance authorized the transfer of $3.5 million for interim financing purposes.

As part of its finding to support the appropriation ordinance, the City determined that the appropriation was not a "project" for purposes of environmental review. This finding supported the city's determination that an EIR was not required by California law.

Henderson was not persuaded by the city's reasoning. A month after the city acted, he filed a second lawsuit, *Mailhot II*, challenging the city's action. He claimed that the appropriation ordinance was a "project," and that the city had violated California law in not preparing an EIR. He also claimed that the appropriation ordinance violated the city charter's "balanced budget" requirements.

But Henderson fared no better in *Mailhot II*. In July 1999, the superior court rejected his claims in *Mailhot II*. While this case was pending in the superior court, the Fourth District Court of Appeal rejected Henderson's claims advanced in *Mailhot I*. Undeterred by his losses, Henderson filed *Mailhot III* in superior court challenging the appropriation ordinance for violating "certain City Charter provisions."

The opponents of the ballpark shifted tactics while *Mailhot III* was pending in superior court. Two citizens, Messrs. Dunkl and Zoebisch, filed a notice of intent to circulate an initiative petition declaring that the conditions of Proposition C had not been met and that the city's obligations should be terminated. They wanted a public vote on their claim to kill the project.

In 2000, the city and the Padres responded to the citizen-demand for a public vote by becoming plaintiffs. In *City of San Diego v. Dunkl*, the plaintiffs asked the superior court to prevent the citizens' initiative from being placed on the ballot. Henderson, you might have guessed, was lurking in the wings. Messrs. Dunkl and Zoebisch were represented by him.

The superior court sided with the city and the Padres on the theory that the factual findings in the citizens' initiative were administrative in nature. It reasoned that only legislative matters are subject to the initiative process. Henderson did not like the result, so he appealed this adverse subject-matter determination to the California Fourth District Court of Appeal.

In a written opinion, the court of appeal affirmed the superior court's decision.[6] It held that, while the reserved power of initiative and referendum were protected by the California Constitution[7] and that the power was to be liberally construed, the power could be exercised only with respect to matters strictly legislative in character. Because the administrative determinations proposed in the citizens' initiative were not properly within the scope of the initiative and referendum process, Henderson again struck out.

The initiative-referendum process had captured Henderson's fancy. In 2000, Henderson sought to place a referendum on the ballot to repeal the bond ordinance. He submitted the referendum to the city clerk on the last day available to submit matters for inclusion on the ballot. After being told that the petitions would be accepted provisionally, subject to verification of their validity, Henderson chose not to leave the petitions with the city clerk's office. It is not clear why he did not leave the petitions supporting the referendum. What is clear, however, is that Henderson continued his efforts to collect voter signatures.

Within a week of submitting the "Bond Ordinance Referendum," Henderson sued the city, the Padres, and others in *Zoebisch v. Abdelnour*. His complaint alleged that the referendum was valid, properly submitted, and should be placed on the ballot. The superior court rejected Henderson's claim, and the superior court's decision was affirmed by the Fourth District Court of Appeal. It reasoned that the referendum had not been filed in a timely manner in accordance with the San Diego Municipal Code.

In 2000, the city enacted an ordinance authorizing the

---

6. City of San Diego v. Dunkl, 103 Cal. Rptr. 2d 269 (Ct. App. 2001).
7. CAL. CONST. art. IV, § 1.

issuance of $299 million in bonds to finance its contribution. Henderson sued the city and the Padres to invalidate the appropriation ordinance in *Currie v. City of San Diego*. He argued that bonding authorization exceeded the Proposition C funding cap of $225 million, as well as the 1999 Annual Appropriation Ordinance.

But the superior court again disagreed with Henderson. It found that the $299 million bond ordinance did not exceed the Proposition C funding cap or the MOU. As written, Proposition C allowed the city to incur a gross debt in excess of $225 million as long as the net amount contributed to the ballpark was limited to the $225 million cap.

The court also determined that because the ballpark would not be completed during the 1999-2000 fiscal year, the city's $225 million contribution would not have to be paid in its entirety during that year. Therefore, it did not violate the city's balanced budget requirement. Finally, the court determined that the mandatory disclosure provisions of the city charter did not apply to the Padres. The charter requires that disclosure of the interests of all persons "applying or bargaining therefor" property or contract rights from the city.

The city and Padres prevailed in *Currie v. City of San Diego*. Henderson once again appealed the adverse determination to the Fourth District Court of Appeal. In March 2001, the court of appeal affirmed the trial court's substantive and procedural determinations in *Currie*. Henderson was not, however, out of legal ammunition.

In 2001, Henderson sued the city, Moores, and others in *Skane v. City of San Diego*. He alleged that the city's "business transactions" with Moores were void because of prohibited conflicts of interest involving gifts made by Moores to members of the city council; the city's obligations under Proposition C; the expiration of the memorandum of understanding; and the invalidity, under the San Diego City Charter, of the resolution authorizing $10 million in interim financing for the ballpark project. Henderson also alleged Moores had violated the Cartwright Act[8] and the Racketeering Influenced and Corrupt Organizations Act (RICO) and had committed unfair business practices. Henderson also recorded three *lis pendens* against property being acquired for the ballpark project.

In 2001, the superior court rejected Henderson's claims in *Skane* on the ground that Moores's actions were protected by the *Noerr-Pennington* doctrine.[9] The court also expunged the lis pendens because Henderson's complaint in *Skane* did not affect the title to or possession of real property. The court entered judgment in favor of the defendants, and Henderson duly appealed the trial court's rulings to the Fourth District Court of Appeal.

Additional litigation was brought by Henderson to stop the project without success.

The Padres Go on the Legal Offense

Strategic Lawsuits Against Public Participation (SLAPP)[10] are generally brought by large private interests to deter citizens from exercising their political or legal rights of free speech or petitioning government to redress grievances or to punish them for exercising those rights. SLAPP lawsuits are used as a weapon to intimidate public opposition to development projects.

---

8. The Cartwright Act is California's basic antitrust law. *See* CAL. BUS. & PROF. CODE § 16720 (Deering 2007).

9. The *Noerr-Pennington* doctrine derives from the First Amendment's guarantee of "the right of the people . . . to petition the Government for a redress of grievances." U.S. CONST. amend. I. This doctrine, which is based on two Supreme Court cases, provides a First Amendment antitrust defense for competitors who petition to influence government action.

10. A Strategic Lawsuit Against Public Participation (SLAPP) is intended to intimidate and silence opponents by burdening them with the cost of legal defense to encourage them to abandon their objections.

In January 2002, Moores sued Henderson for malicious prosecution. The tort of malicious prosecution may be a disguised type of SLAPP suit because it has the potential to impose an undue "chilling effect" on the ordinary citizen's willingness to bring a civil dispute to a court. As a consequence, the tort is carefully circumscribed so that litigants with potentially valid claims are not deterred from bringing their legal claims.

Many states have adopted anti-SLAPP statutes, which endeavor to protect a citizen's right to bring legal claims. Henderson brought a motion to strike Moores's malicious prosecution lawsuit based on his contention that the suit violated California's anti-SLAPP law. This law provides:

> A cause of action against a person arising from any act
> of that person in furtherance of the person's right of petition or free speech under the United States or California
> Constitution in connection with a public issue shall be
> subject to a special motion to strike, unless the court

determines that the plaintiff has established that there is a probability that the plaintiff will prevail on the claim.

The anti-SLAPP statute is designed to encourage citizens to participate in matters of public significance by allowing a trial court to promptly dismiss unmeritorious actions or claims that are brought to chill the valid exercise of another's rights. Simply stated, the motion to strike provides an expeditious procedural mechanism to dismiss unmeritorious claims at an early stage of the litigation.

Applying the Anti-SLAPP Statute

If Henderson could show that his lawsuits furthered his right to petition or to free speech in connection with "a public issue," the burden would then shift to Moores to demonstrate "a probability" that he would prevail on the merits of the malicious prosecution at trial.

The trial court denied Henderson's motion to strike. He appealed the denial of the motion to the Fourth District Court of Appeal. He argued that he was absolutely privileged to file his lawsuits, and thus could not be sued for malicious prosecution. The court of appeal found that Henderson had enjoyed no absolute privilege to file the underlying actions.

Henderson also argued that Moores had not met the statutory burden of showing a probability of success. In order to demonstrate the probability of success, Moores had to demonstrate three things to the court. First, Moores had to show that he prevailed in the lawsuits brought by Henderson. Second, Moores had to show that Henderson's lawsuits were brought without a "legally tenable" basis. The standard for making the determination that the claims were tenable is whether a "reasonable attorney" would consider the lawsuits "legally arguable." Finally,

Moores had to show that the lawsuits were initiated with an improper motive, namely with malice. The evidence had to show that Henderson deliberately misused the legal system for personal gain or satisfaction at the expense of the wrongfully sued defendant.

The court of appeal found that Moores had produced sufficient evidence to avoid Henderson's anti-SLAPP defense in the *Currie* case. This finding did not mean that Moores's underlying claim was valid. The merits of the malicious prosecution were to be determined at trial.

With respect to the rest of the anti-SLAPP litigation, Moores lost. Therefore, Henderson's motion to strike was granted as to the other claims advanced by Moores and the Padres. In *Mailhot III* and *Zoebisch*, Moores had not met the statutory burden of establishing a probability of success, and thus the motion to strike was granted as to those claims.

What happened on remand is unknown to this author. Presumably, there was a settlement of some sort.

Some Broader Lessons

Project proponents may suffer damage as a result of litigation designed to defeat a ballpark project. Of course, the proponents may recover their costs of litigation should the matter be terminated in their favor. But they also may seek to recover consequential damages through litigation using any one of a number of theories, including malicious prosecution.

The *Padres v. Henderson* case illustrates the application of the anti-SLAPP statute. The fact that the *Currie* case did not warrant the application of this statute may provide the precedent for discouraging citizens from using litigation to limit governmental action they think is wrong. A corollary to this point is that private partnerships with government may feel less constrained to follow the rules of the game.

An alternative approach to malicious prosecution litigation is to contractually allocate the risk of loss from opponent-litigation at the time the parties enter into the ballpark agreements. The availability of a tort remedy may ultimately work to the detriment of the public by chilling the free exercise of the right to protest government action.

Umpire's Ruling

Delays and Appeals

Litigation—whether about ballparks or other matters—can be a lengthy process, but umpires decide disputes quickly. And, while the appellate process brings uniformity to law, it also delays the resolution of legal disputes. The Rules of Baseball address delay during a game, and they also create an "appellate" process to provide quick answers when needed.

If a team fails to show up on time or does not start play within five minutes after the umpire calls "play," the game may be forfeited to the opposing team; the same power exists if a team "[e]mploys tactics palpably designed to delay or shorten a game."[1] When it is the batter's turn, the batter must "promptly" enter the batter's box.[2] If the batter refuses, the umpire may call a strike.[3] When no runners are on base, the pitcher is required to pitch within 12 seconds of receiving the ball with the batter " in the box, alert to the pitcher."[4]

If a manager believes that the umpire has made an erroneous call, the manager may protest the game only if the mistake regards the meaning of the rules. Disagreements about the facts—for example, whether a runner beat the ball to the bag or tagged the base—cannot be the subject of a protest. This limit to questions about the rules screens out the vast majority of disputes over umpires' calls. When the dispute does focus on the rules, the protesting manager must inform the umpire of the protest before "the next pitch, play or attempted play"; this step gives the umpire one last chance to get the rules right before proceeding with the game. If the protesting team goes on to win the game notwithstanding the alleged Rules violation, the protest is withdrawn.[5] And so very few protests get to the stage of actually being considered by the MLB President's Office, and those are handled promptly.

When a protest is upheld after the completion of the game, the usual remedy is to replay the game from the point of the

mistake, correcting it and playing the game out from that point. This remedy is not usually available in law, of course; the harm complained about in court often cannot simply be waved away, and courts often need to use substitutes (like money damages) to redress the harm. But restarting a game is not a perfect remedy either. At the time the game is replayed, one team may have lost players to injury or trade, and pitching staffs may be more or less well rested than they would have been if the game had proceeded initially without the mistake; replaying a game among other regularly scheduled games increases the advantage for the team with a stronger bench and deeper pitching staff. But some harms are simply too difficult to rectify—at least on a baseball field.

---

1. Rules 4.15(a)–(b). Delaying tactics can shorten the number of innings played in a game, for example, when a team believes that a new inning cannot begin after a certain time because of a curfew or impending bad weather.
2. Rule 6.02(a).
3. Rule 6.02(c).
4. Rule 8.04.
5. Rule 4.19.

Up for Grabs?

Alex Popov v. Patrick Hayashi,
2002 WL 31833731 (Cal. Superior)[1]

Baseball fans realize that a home run baseball may be valuable. Mark McGwire's record-setting 70th home run ball, for example, fetched a handsome $2.7 million. Thus, it is not surprising that spectators at baseball games often madly scramble to become the owner of their piece of baseball history.

The dash to become the owner of a home run ball may generate legal controversy, and *Popov* may be the most famous litigated case on the subject. The case, which received national and international attention, deals with the competing claims by two spectators to ownership of Barry Bonds's 73rd home run ball. The ball is part of baseball history because it set the single-season record for homeruns.

The ownership of baseballs used in professional baseball games is initially straightforward. The home team buys the baseballs, puts them in play, and generally controls their use during the game. As the owner of the baseball, the home team could demand the return of the ball once it leaves the field of play.

But the home team effectively abandons its legal claim to

---

1. *Available at* http://fl1.findlaw.com/news.findlaw.com/hdocs/docs/bonds/popov hayashi121802dec.pdf (last visited Sept. 28, 2008).

recover home run balls once they are hit into the stands. This customary practice, which is sometimes stated and at other times implied, is to allow the lucky fan who takes "possession" of the prize to keep it. Teams realize that the goodwill earned by allowing a lucky fan to keep the home run ball outweighs the ill will that would be associated with demanding its return. Teams don't want the notoriety of being seen wrestling the ball from the grasp of a fan. It would be bad for business.

The application of legal theory of "possession" can affect the outcome of the dispute between two fans both claiming to be the possessor of the prized ball. But the facts are also important.

The legal controversy in *Popov* arose from events occurring on the last day of the 2001 baseball season. The San Francisco Giants were playing the Los Angeles Dodgers at Pac-Bell Park (now AT&T Park), the home of the Giants. Dennis Springer, who was pitching for the Dodgers, advanced the count against Barry Bonds to 3 balls and 2 strikes in the bottom of the first inning. Springer threw Bonds a 43-mile-per-hour knuckleball.[2] Bonds met the knuckler with a 380-foot blast into the right-field stands. It was Bonds 73rd home run ball and set the single-season record for homeruns.

Alex Popov stood on the walkway waiting and monitoring the game on the earbud to his radio. He was stationed perfectly in the standing room only arcade section near right field. With his outstretched mitt, Popov "caught" Bonds's blast in the top part of his glove's webbing. Josh Keppel, an on-the-scene cameraman, captured his "snow-cone catch" on videotape. He also recorded the ensuing melee of those after the same souvenir.

---

2. When originally developed as a pitch, the knuckleball (commonly called a knuckler) was gripped by the pitcher with his knuckles, and hence its name. Today, different grips may be used to produce the knuckleball. The effect, however, is the same. The flight of the ball has an erratic, unpredictable motion because the spin of the ball is minimized.

The videotape is not clear as to whether Popov had actual control of the ball before he was mobbed by the other fans shoving and grabbing for the same prize. Several things, however, were clear from the videotape. First, the ball came loose from Popov's mitt during the melee. Second, Patrick Hayashi picked up the ball and had actual possession of it when the scrum in the mosh pit ended. Third, the mob "engaged in violent and illegal behavior" in frenzied pursuit of the ball. Fourth, Hayashi was not part of the mob and committed no wrongful act. He simply picked up the loose ball, put it in his pocket, and then claimed to be the lucky owner.

The Law

Popov had a different view as to ownership of the prized ball. He sued Hayashi for conversion and "trespass to chattel."[3] Popov was covering his legal bases by using both theories.

To establish a case of conversion, the plaintiff must prove that the defendant interfered with the plaintiff's possession or right to possession of an item of personal property. The interference must be judged serious enough to justify requiring the defendant to pay the plaintiff the full value of the property. Wrongfully refusing to return the personal property to the owner, for example, would constitute an act of conversion. The longer a defendant withholds the item and the more extensive its interference with the rights of the owner, the more likely it is that a claim of conversion will be sustained.

Trespass to chattel, historically known as *trespass de bonis asportatis*, also protects an owner's right of possession. When the interference with possession is not particularly serious, the

---

3. The word "chattel" is used by lawyers to describe personal property, and is historically derived from the reference to "cattle."

theory of trespass to chattel applies. If a plaintiff is temporarily deprived of possession by a defendant, this theory applies. The plaintiff in such a case would be entitled to actual damages for the dispossession and not the full value of the property.

In order to establish the claim of conversion or trespass to chattel, Popov had to prove that he had actual possession of the ball or the right to its possession. As a legal concept, possession requires both the intent to control the property and a certain amount of actual control of it. Popov's actions, as evidenced by the videotape, clearly showed that he intended to possess the ball. But intent alone is not enough. He also had to prove that he had done enough to actually reduce the ball to his control.

In resolving the control issue, the court adopted what it referred to as Gray's rule:

> A person who catches a baseball that enters the stands is its owner. A ball is caught if the person has achieved complete control of the ball at the point in time that the momentum of the ball and the momentum of the fan while attempting to catch the ball ceases. A baseball, which is dislodged by incidental contact with an inanimate object or another person, before momentum has ceased, is not possessed. Incidental contact with another person is contact that is not intended by the other person. The first person to pick up a loose ball and secure it becomes its possessor.[4]

The central idea of Gray's rule is that the actor must retain control of the ball after "incidental contact." Bobbling the ball doesn't count.

Although the court recognized that some case precedent

---

4. Named after Professor Brian Gray, Univ. of Cal., Hastings College of Law.

supports the view that a person who is in the process of gaining actual possession and control may receive the right to complete the process without interference by others, the court was not persuaded that this approach should be followed. According to the court, it would be "unworkable and unreasonable" in the context of this case. Because it is physically possible to acquire unequivocal dominion and control of a baseball before claiming possession, the controlling rule should be consistent with this possibility.

But Equity Rules

The evidence did not support the conclusion that Popov would have retained control of the ball after the "incidental contact." Thus, it was not convincingly demonstrated that he had full control of the ball. But the reason he did not have full control was that he was mobbed. As a matter of fundamental fairness, the court reasoned, Popov should have been given the chance to complete the catch unimpeded by the stampeding mob, which the court likened to a "gang of bandits."

Popov did not have full possession. Nevertheless, he had a "qualified right to possession" and this qualified right enabled him to pursue his conversion claim. As a matter of policy, failure to protect this interest would be tantamount to encouraging mob behavior to shake the ball loose.

But what of Hayashi's fairness claim? He was not a wrongdoer. Rather, he also was a victim of the mob. He did everything necessary to claim full possession of the ball. The legal dilemma was clear: Awarding the ball to Popov would be unfair to Hayashi, and awarding it to Hayashi would be unfair to Popov.

Both Popov and Hayashi had claims of equal merit to the ball. In a move patented by Alexander the Great, the Gordian legal knot was severed by recognizing the undivided, equal interest in the prize. The ball, the court found, was encumbered by Popov's qualified pre-possessory interest, which should be recognized through the application of the concept of equitable division. Popov's claim of conversion was sustained, but only to the extent needed to protect his equal and undivided interest in the ball. Based on this reasoning, the court concludes, "the ball must be sold and the proceeds divided equally between the parties."

Some general principles can be stated. A spectator, who has the ball in his or her glove, has the right to secure full possession without the interference by other fans. That is essentially what the court held. Calling "it's mine" as the ball sails into the stands or simply touching the ball is not enough. There has to be a certain amount of actual control by the claimant. Although *Popov* seeks to promote civilized, nonviolent fan behavior in the scramble for a home run ball, it is doubtful it will have this effect. Darwinian principles will continue to apply.

The Taxman Cometh

What are the tax consequences of selling the valuable ball? It is arguably functionally similar to finding "treasure," which is taxable under section 61 of the Internal Revenue Code.[5] This section broadly defines a taxpayer's "gross income" to include "all income from whatever source derived." Thus, the lucky fan might also be the recipient of a tax bill.

In 1998, the Internal Revenue Service provided a brief explanation of the basic income and gift tax principles that would apply to a baseball fan who catches a home run ball and immediately returns it, which was not the case in *Popov*.

---

5. 26 U.S.C. § 61 (2006); *see also* Rev. Rul. 61, 1953-1 Cum. Bull. 17 [what is included in gross income].

In general, the fan would not have taxable income when the ball is returned based on an analogy to principles of tax law that apply when a person immediately declines a prize or returns unsolicited merchandise. Likewise, no gift tax would be owed. Commenting on this situation, then-IRS Commissioner Charles O. Rossotti said, "Sometimes pieces of the tax code can be as hard to understand as the infield fly rule. All I know is that the fan who gives back the home run ball deserves a round of applause, not a big tax bill." It is strange that the commissioner would think the infield fly rule can be as hard to understand as the tax code. It's not even a close call.

The Market Value of Baseball Memorabilia

The actual market value of baseball memorabilia is tied to the legitimacy of the record. In 2006, baseball commissioner Bud Selig asked former Senator George Mitchell to investigate steroid use and other performance enhancing drugs in professional baseball. On December 13, 2007, he released the Mitchell Report. Among other things, the report casts a dark shadow on recent baseball records, and is apt to directly affect the market value of tainted record-setting baseballs.

Bonds's place in baseball history, and thus the value of his historic setting home run ball, may be tarnished by the outcome of his criminal indictment in the U.S. District Court, Northern District of California. The case has not yet been decided at this time, so the presumption of innocence applies.

```
1   SCOTT N. SCHOOLS (SCBN 9990)
2   United States Attorney

3                                                    FILED
4
                                                     NOV 1 5 2007
5                      E-filing
                                          RICHARD W. WIEKING
6                                    CLERK, U.S. DISTRICT COURT
                                  NORTHERN DISTRICT OF CALIFORNIA
7
8                   UNITED STATES DISTRICT COURT
9                 NORTHERN DISTRICT OF CALIFORNIA                WHA
10                    SAN FRANCISCO DIVISION

11                                          CR 07         0732
12  UNITED STATES OF AMERICA,      )    No.
                                   )
13          Plaintiff,             )    VIOLATIONS: 18 U.S.C. § 1623(a) –
                                   )    Perjury; 18 U.S.C. § 1503 – Obstruction of
14  v.                             )    Justice
                                   )
15                                 )    SAN FRANCISCO VENUE
    BARRY LAMAR BONDS,             )
16                                 )
            Defendant.             )
17  ───────────────────────────────)

18
19                          INDICTMENT
20  The Grand Jury charges:
21          Background
22          At all times relevant to this Indictment:
23          1.      The defendant, BARRY LAMAR BONDS ("Bonds"), was a Major League
24  Baseball player for the San Francisco Giants.
25          2.      Balco Laboratories, Inc. ("Balco"), was a California corporation performing
26  blood-testing, among other functions.  Balco was located in Burlingame, California.
27          3.      Greg Anderson ("Anderson") was a personal athletic trainer whose clients
28  included numerous professional athletes, including Bonds.  Anderson was affiliated with Balco

    INDICTMENT
```

94

1 in that, among other things, he: obtained illegal drugs for later distribution to his clients

2 (including professional athletes); submitted biological specimens from his clients to Balco for

3 testing (including sending the specimens off to outside laboratories for analysis); and obtained

4 the laboratory analysis results of those specimens from Balco.

5   4.   A federal criminal investigation ("the criminal investigation"), led by the Internal

6 Revenue Service-Criminal Investigation Division ("IRS-CID"), commenced in the Northern

7 District of California concerning Balco's distribution of anabolic steroids and other illegal

8 performance-enhancing drugs and the related money laundering of proceeds from the drug

9 distributions. The criminal investigation initially resulted in an indictment and the convictions of

10 four defendants on federal charges, including illegal drug distribution and money laundering

11 offenses.

12   5.   One focus of the criminal investigation, among others, concerned whether Balco,

13 Anderson, and others were engaged in illegal drug distribution and money laundering arising

14 from distributions of illegal drugs to professional athletes and others.

15   6.   As part of the criminal investigation, on or about September 3, 2003, federal

16 search warrants, issued in the Northern District of California, were executed. Among other

17 things, investigators obtained evidence concerning Bonds and his relationship with Anderson and

18 Balco.

19   7.   As part of the criminal investigation, several professional athletes, including but

20 not limited to Bonds, along with other witnesses, were subpoenaed before the Federal Grand Jury

21 to provide, among other things, testimony about their knowledge and involvement with Balco

22 and its employees, including but not limited to Victor Conte and James Valente, as well as any

23 relationship with Anderson.

24   8.   On or about December 4, 2003, Bonds testified before the Grand Jury. Bonds

25 received an Order of Immunity for his Grand Jury testimony, pursuant to 18 U.S.C. § 6003 and

26 28 C.F.R. § 0.175, and was informed that pursuant to that order neither his testimony nor any

27 information directly or indirectly derived from his testimony could be used against him in any

28 criminal case except a prosecution for perjury, false declaration, or otherwise failing to comply

INDICTMENT   2

1   with the Court's order.

2   9.   During the criminal investigation, evidence was obtained including positive tests

3   for the presence of anabolic steroids and other performance-enhancing substances for Bonds and

4   other professional athletes.

5   COUNT ONE: (18 U.S.C. § 1623(a) – Perjury)

6   10.   The factual allegations contained in paragraphs one through nine above are

7   incorporated herein as if set forth in full.

8   11.   On or about December 4, 2003, in the Northern District of California, the

9   defendant,

10   BARRY LAMAR BONDS,

11   having taken an oath to testify truthfully in a proceeding before a Grand Jury sitting in the

12   Northern District of California, unlawfully, willfully, knowingly, and contrary to such oath, did

13   make false material declarations, that is, he gave the following underlined false testimony:

14   Q: I know the answer - - let me ask you this again. I know we kind of got the into

15   this. Let me be real clear about this. Did he [Anderson] ever give you anything that you

16   knew to be a steroid? Did he ever give a steroid?

17   A: I don't think Greg would do anything like that to me and jeopardize our

18   friendship. I just don't think he would do that.

19   Q: Well, when you say you don't think he would do that, to your knowledge, I mean,

20   did you ever take any steroids that he gave you?

21   (a)   A: Not that I know of.

22   ********************************

23   Q: Okay. So, I got to ask, Mr. Bonds. There's this number associated on a document

24   with your name, and corresponding to Barry B. on the other document, and it does have

25   these two listed anabolic steroids as testing positive in connection with it. Do you follow

26   my question?

27   A: I follow where you're going, yeah.

28   Q: So, I guess I got to ask the question again, I mean, did you take steroids? And

INDICTMENT   3

1   specifically this test the is in November of 2000. So, I'm going to ask you in the weeks

2   and months leading up to November 2000, were you taking steroids - -

3   (b)   A: No.

4   Q: - - or anything like that?

5   (c)   A: No, I wasn't at all. I've never seen these documents. I've never seen these

6   papers.

7   ********************************

8   Q: So, starting in December 2001, on this page, again, there's BB here, which

9   obviously are consistent with your initials; correct?

10   A: He could know other BBs.

11   Q: Correct.

12   But BB would also be your initials; is that correct.

13   A: That's correct.

14   ********************************

15   Q: Okay. Were you obtaining testosterone from Mr. Anderson during this period of

16   time?

17   (d)   A: Not at all.

18   ********************************

19   Q: In January 2001 were you taking either the flax seed oil or the cream?

20   A: No.

21   Q: And were you taking any other steroids?

22   (e)   A: No.

23   All in violation of Title 18, United States Code, Section 1623(a).

24   ///

25   ///

26   ///

27   ///

28   ///

INDICTMENT   4

97

1	<u>COUNT TWO</u>: (18 U.S.C. § 1623(a) – Perjury)
2	12. The factual allegations contained in paragraphs one through nine above are
3	incorporated herein as if set forth in full.
4	13. On or about December 4, 2003, in the Northern District of California, the
5	defendant,
6	BARRY LAMAR BONDS,
7	having taken an oath to testify truthfully in a proceeding before a Grand Jury sitting in the
8	Northern District of California, unlawfully, willfully, knowingly, and contrary to such oath, did
9	make false material declarations, that is, he gave the following underlined false testimony:
10	Q: Did Greg ever give you anything that required a syringe to inject yourself with?
11	A: I've only had one doctor touch me. And that's my only personal doctor.
12	Greg, like I said, we don't get into each others' personal lives. We're friends, but I don't
13	– we don't sit around and talk baseball, because he knows I don't want – don't come to
14	my house talking baseball. If you want to come to my house and talk about fishing, some
15	other stuff, we'll be good friends. You come around talking about baseball, you go on. I
16	don't talk about his business. You know what I mean?
17	*********************************
18	Q: So no one else other than perhaps the team doctor and your personal physician has
19	ever injected anything in to you or taken anything out?
20	A: Well, there's other doctors from surgeries. I can answer that question, if you're
21	getting technical like that. Sure, there are other people that have stuck needles in me and
22	have drawn out - - I've had a bunch of surgeries, yes.
23	Q: So - -
24	A: So sorry.
25	Q: - - the team physician, when you've had surgery, and your own personal
26	physician. But no other individuals like Mr. Anderson or any associates of his?
27	(a) A: <u>No, no.</u>
28	*******************************

INDICTMENT   5

1 Q: And, again, I guess we've covered this, but - - and did he [Anderson] ever give

2 you anything that he told you had to be taken with a needle or syringe?

3 A: Greg wouldn't do that. He knows I'm against that stuff. So, he would never

4 come up to me - - he would never jeopardize our friendship like that.

5 Q: Okay. So, just so I'm clear, the answer is no to that, he never gave you anything

6 like that?

7 (b) A: <u>Right.</u>

8 All in violation of Title 18, United States Code, Section 1623(a).

9 <u>COUNT THREE</u>: (18 U.S.C. § 1623(a) – Perjury)

10 14.   The factual allegations contained in paragraphs one through nine above are

11 incorporated herein as if set forth in full.

12 15.   On or about December 4, 2003, in the Northern District of California, the

13 defendant,

14 BARRY LAMAR BONDS,

15 having taken an oath to testify truthfully in a proceeding before a Grand Jury sitting in the

16 Northern District of California, unlawfully, willfully, knowingly, and contrary to such oath, did

17 make false material declarations, that is, he gave the following underlined false testimony:

18 Q: All right. Did Greg ever talk to you or give you anything called human growth

19 hormone?

20 (a) A: <u>No.</u>

21 *********************************

22 Q: And, again, just to be clear and then I'll leave it, but he [Anderson] never gave

23 you anything that you understood to be human growth hormone? Did he ever give you

24 anything like that?

25 (b) A: <u>No.</u>

26 *********************************

27 Q: And were you obtaining growth hormone from Mr. Anderson?

28 (c) A: <u>Not at all.</u>

INDICTMENT   6

1   ********************************

2   Q: In January of 2002, then, again, just to be clear, you weren't getting any

3   testosterone or growth hormone from Mr. Anderson during that period of time?

4 (d)   A: <u>No.</u>

5   All in violation of Title 18, United States Code, Section 1623(a).

6 <u>COUNT FOUR</u>: (18 U.S.C. § 1623(a) – Perjury)

7   16.   The factual allegations contained in paragraphs one through nine above are

8 incorporated herein as if set forth in full.

9   17.   On or about December 4, 2003, in the Northern District of California, the

10 defendant,

11   BARRY LAMAR BONDS,

12 having taken an oath to testify truthfully in a proceeding before a Grand Jury sitting in the

13 Northern District of California, unlawfully, willfully, knowingly, and contrary to such oath, did

14 make false material declarations, that is, he gave the following underlined false testimony:

15   Q: Let me ask the same question about Greg at this point, we'll go into this in a little

16   bit more detail, but did you ever get anything else from Greg besides advice or tips on

17   your weight lifting and also the vitamins and the proteins that you already referenced?

18   A: This year, in 2003 - - at the end of 2002, 2003 season, when I was going through -

19   - my dad died of cancer, you know, and everyone knows that.

20   Q: Yes. I'm sorry about that.

21   A: And everyone tries to give me everything. You got companies that provide us

22   with more junk to try than anything. And you know that as well.

23   I was fatigued, tired, just needed recovery, you know. And this guy says: "Try

24   this cream, try this cream." And Greg came to the ballpark and he said, you know: "This

25   will help you recover," and he rubbed some cream on my arm, like, some lotion-type

26   stuff, and, like, gave me some flax seed oil, that's what he called it, called it some flax

27   seed oil, man. It's, like: " Whatever, dude."

28   And I was at the ballpark, whatever, I don't care. What's lotion going to do to

INDICTMENT   7

1			me? How many times have I heard that: "This is going to rub into you and work." Let
2			him be happy. We're friends. You know?
3		Q:	When did that happen for the first time?
4	(a)	A:	Not until 2003, this season.
5			********************************
6		Q:	And - - all right. So, how many times approximately do you think you got these
7			tubes with what Mr. Anderson told you was flax seed oil?
8		A:	Maybe once a home stand or something, if that. Greg didn't travel with me on the
9			road. So, I was at home, when I came home.
10		Q:	And the first time was the beginning of this year's season, in 2003?
11	(b)	A:	Yes, 2003, because I was battling with the problems with my father and the - - just
12			the lack of sleep, lack of everything.
13			********************************
14		Q:	Mr. Anderson had never given you anything or asked you to take anything before
15			the 2003 season; is that right?
16		A:	We never had those discussions. We don't discuss about his -- you know, part of
17			his world of business is his business. My business is my business. So, we don't --
18		Q:	I'm asking --
19		A:	No.
20		Q:	That's not my question. My question is - -
21		A:	No.
22		Q:	- - prior to the last season, you never took anything that he asked you to take, other
23			than vitamins?
24	(c)	A:	Right. We didn't have any other discussions.
25		Q:	No oils like this or anything like this before?
26	(d)	A:	No, no, no, not at all. Not at all.
27			********************************
28		Q:	Okay. So, first of all, Mr. Bonds, I guess I want to recheck with you or ask you

INDICTMENT   8

1 again exactly when you started getting the - - what I'll call the recovery items, what you
2 understood to be flax seed oil and the cream, when you started getting that from Greg
3 Anderson. I think that you said - - but please correct me if I'm wrong - - that you thought
4 it was prior to this current baseball season.
5 But let me ask, I mean, is it possible it's actually a year before, after the 2000 - -
6 well, actually two years before, after the 2001 season? Because this first calendar is dated
7 December 2001 with "BB" on it and its got a number of entries that I'd like to ask you
8 about.
9 Were you getting items during that period of time from Greg?
10 (e) A: No. Like I said, I don't recall having anything like this at all during that time of
11   year. It was toward the end of 2000, after the World Series, you know, when my father
12   was going through cancer.
13   **********************************
14   Q: In December 2001.
15   And what about the - - the clear - - either the clear or the cream, were you getting
16   either of those substances in December of 2001 from Mr. Anderson?
17 (f) A: No. Like I said, I recall it being toward the end of 2002 - - 2002, after 2002
18   season.
19   Q: Okay.
20 (g) A: And that's what I recall.
21   **********************************
22   Q: And you weren't getting this flax seed oil stuff during that period of time [January
23   2002]?
24 (h) A: Not that I can recall. Like I say, I could be wrong. But I'm - - I'm - - going from
25   my recollection it was, like, in the 2002 time and 2003 season.
26   All in violation of Title 18, United States Code, Section 1623(a).
27 ///
28 ///

INDICTMENT   9

102

COUNT FIVE: (18 U.S.C. § 1503 – Obstruction of Justice)

18. The factual allegations contained in paragraphs one through nine above are incorporated herein as if set forth in full.

19. On or about December 4, 2003, in the Northern District of California, and elsewhere, the defendant,

BARRY LAMAR BONDS,

unlawfully, willfully, and knowingly, did corruptly endeavor to influence, obstruct, and impede the due administration of justice, by knowingly giving Grand Jury testimony that was intentionally evasive, false, and misleading, that is:

    (a) The false statements made by the defendant as charged in Counts 1-4 of this indictment; and

    (b) Evasive and misleading testimony.

All in violation of Title 18, United States Code, Section 1503.

DATED: *Nov 15, 2007*

A TRUE BILL.

FOREPERSON

SCOTT N. SCHOOLS
United States Attorney

BRIAN J. STRETCH
Chief, Criminal Division

(Approved as to form:)
AUSA PARRELLA

INDICTMENT   10

Umpire's Ruling

What is a Catch?

Just as it was critical to determine what
act constituted the gaining of possession of
the Bonds home run ball, so too is it important to determine
what counts as a catch on the field of play. A fly ball that hits
the glove of one defensive player and is grabbed by another
defensive player before it hits the ground counts. It doesn't
count, however, if the ball bounces off a defensive player and
hits the outfield wall, an offensive player, or an umpire before
being caught by a defensive player. Nor is it a catch if the
defensive player seems to catch the ball but, "simultaneously
or immediately following his contact with the ball, he collides
with a player or with a wall" or "falls down, and as a result
of such collision or falling, drops the ball."[1]

   In the case of a juggling or multi-player "catch," a base runner
who is tagging up is allowed to leave base as soon as the ball is
first touched by a defensive player.[2] Otherwise, a clever and
dexterous outfielder could juggle the ball all the way from the
warning track to the infield to prevent a base runner from
advancing on an out.

---

1. Rule 2.00 (definition of "catch").
2. Comment to Rule 2.00 (catch).

Stadium Liability for Spectator Injuries

Benejam v. Detroit Tigers, Inc., 246 Mich. App. 645, 635 N.W.2d 219 (Mich. Ct. App. 2001)[1]

Hundreds of reported cases deal with spectators getting injured at baseball games. Some litigation is against the baseball player who caused the injury, such as when the player carelessly throws a bat that injures a spectator. Other cases are brought against the ballpark owner or operator. Whether the ballpark owner or operator is found liable most frequently turns on whether the court finds that the defendant owes the plaintiff a legal duty to protect against the particular risk of harm.

In the early years of the game, the area directly behind home plate was a particularly dangerous place for spectators. Ballpark operators quickly realized that they were in the business of providing fans with entertainment and not with emergency medical services. This realization, combined with the threat of financial liability, encouraged them to take safety seriously by providing protective screens.

---

1. *Available at* http://courtofappeals.mijud.net/documents/OPINIONS/FINAL/COA/ 20060817_C267321_38_267321.OPN.PDF (last visited Sept, 28, 2008).

In 1913, the Missouri Court of Appeal decided *Crane v. Kansas City Baseball & Exhibition Co.*[2] In addition to being one of the earliest reported spectator-injury appellate decisions, it also provides the framework for analyzing such cases. The court upheld the trial court's dismissal of a lawsuit brought by a fan injured by a foul ball during a minor league baseball game. The court reasoned that the risks and dangers incident to the game of baseball are matters of common knowledge. Lawyers would call this "assumption of the risk."[3]

Unusual cases pop up that do not appear to comfortably fit within this theory. Alyssia Maribel Benejam, who was a minor, and her parents were attending a Detroit Tigers game when Alyssia was injured when part of a player's bat broke and hit her, crushing her fingers. Alyssia was sitting "close to the playing field along the third base line" when she was injured.

The Tigers had a safety screen behind home plate that extended down the first-base and third-base lines. Considering the location of plaintiff's seat with reference to the screen and the batter's box, it was, indeed, an unusual and unexpected accident. The broken bat fragment did not come through the screen and, thus, the plaintiff was not injured because the screen was defective or otherwise inadequate. Rather, the injury appeared to have occurred when the bat fragment performed the remarkable feat of taking a sharp turn around the end of the screen.

---

2. Crane v. Kansas City Baseball & Exhibition Co., 153 S.W. 1076 (Mo. Ct. App. 1913).

3. Numerous distracting activities, such as jumbotron monitors, mascots, and vendors pitching bags of peanuts, occur during a game and compete for a spectator's attention. In *Lowe v. California League of Professional Baseball*, 65 Cal. Rptr. 2d 105 (Cal. Ct. App. 1997), the California Fourth District Court of Appeal found that a class "A" minor league baseball team's mascot cavorting in the stands and distracting the plaintiff's attention by bumping into him during a game could constitute negligence by increasing the inherent risk to the plaintiff of being struck by a foul ball. Therefore, the trial court erred in applying primary assumption of the risk principles.

Alyssia and her parents sued the Tigers. They advanced two arguments. First, they claimed that the defendant failed to exercise ordinary care in maintaining the premises in a safe manner. Second, they argued that the defendant failed to provide an adequate warning about flying projectiles, such as the broken bat. The plaintiffs also sued the maker of the broken bat, Hillerich & Bradsby Company,[4] but their claim against the bat company was settled before trial.

At trial, the Tigers argued that they should prevail as a matter of law because the plaintiffs could not and did not present a viable legal claim. The trial court disagreed, and let the jury decide whether the Tigers had exercised "ordinary care" in providing "reasonably safe" premises. The jury found them liable. Alyssia was entitled to a little more than $1 million in damages—$917,000 in noneconomic damages, $56,000 in lost earning capacity, and $35,000 for past and future medical expenses. The Tigers appealed.

The Standard of Care

On appeal, the Tigers confronted the fact that no Michigan law was directly on point. They argued that other states, however, had addressed it and had adopted a "limited-duty rule." According to this approach, an operator's legal duty is satisfied when it provides sufficient screening to protect spectators in the most dangerous areas and provides a sufficient number of seats in those areas. The error of the trial court, the Tigers claimed, was in failing to recognize that their legal duty had been satisfied.

The plaintiffs, not surprisingly, had a different view. They claimed that baseball stadium cases should be governed by the

---

4. Hillerich & Bradsby is most famously known for manufacturing the Louisville Slugger line of bats.

"usual" inviter-invitee principles, not by any limited-duty rule or special "baseball rule." These principles, they argued, establish that the stadium operator owes a duty of reasonable care to them to make the premises safe.

The appellate court adopted the limited-duty rule. This rule protects the stadium operator that provides screening for the most dangerous areas, which includes the area behind home plate, and accommodates those fans who seek protective seating. The screening provided by the Tigers, the court found, was sufficient to meet their legal obligation and, thus, avoid being held liable.

Public policy considerations influenced the court. It found that the limited-duty rule leaves the baseball stadium owner free, without the fear of liability, to accommodate those fans who prefer unobstructed and uninsulated contact with the game. Fear of litigation and liability, in the court's view, would likely require screening far in excess of that preferred by most fans. The Tigers should not be expected to screen most or all of the stadium. In addition, the court reasoned that "the every day reality of attending a baseball game includes subjecting oneself to the risk that a ball or bat might leave the field and cause injury."

The Duty to Warn

Having lost the claim that the premises were unsafe, the plaintiffs next argued that the defendants failed to provide an adequate warning that some object might come off the field and cause injury. The court also rejected this argument. It found that judicial precedent from other states, including Ohio, Missouri, Georgia, California, and Texas, had considered this argument, and had rejected it. The court concluded, "we find these precedents to be compelling and persuasive."

The court additionally found that the limited-duty rule was inconsistent with the duty to warn. The legal premise of the limited-duty rule is that spectators know of the dangers and, because they are open and obvious, no duty exists to warn about them. Finally, the court noted that plaintiffs offered little, if any, evidence to support why the warnings that were given by the Tigers should be found inadequate. Given the nature of the accident, it was not clear whether any type of warning would have made a difference in preventing the injury.

Some states recently have enacted statutes that codify the limited-duty rule applied in *Benejam*. The following statute adopted by Arizona[5] is illustrative:

A. An owner is not liable for injuries to spectators who are struck by baseballs, baseball bats or other equipment used by players during a baseball game unless the owner either:

1. Does not provide protective seating that is reasonably sufficient to satisfy expected requests.

2. Intentionally injures a spectator.

B. This section does not prevent or limit the liability of an owner who fails to maintain the premises of the baseball stadium in a reasonably safe condition.

C. This section does not create an independent duty of care for a registered design professional or licensed contractor.

D. A registered design professional or a licensed contractor who is involved in the design, construction or operation of the facility is not liable for injuries to spectators who are struck by baseballs, baseball bats or

---

5. Ariz. Rev. Stat. Ann. § 12-554 (2006).

111

other equipment used by players during a baseball game unless a registered design professional or a licensed contractor either:

    1. Does not provide for protective seating that is reasonably sufficient to satisfy expected requests.

    2. Intentionally injures a spectator.

    E. This section does not prevent or limit liability of a registered design professional or a licensed contractor who fails to design, construct or operate the premises of the baseball stadium in a reasonably safe condition or manner.

    F. As used in this section:

    1. "Baseball game" means an amateur or professional baseball game, whether for exhibition or competition. Baseball game includes pregame and postgame activities regardless of the time of day when the game is played.

    2. "Owner" means a person, city, town, county, special district, limited liability company, school district, community college district, college or university that is in lawful possession and control of a baseball team or facility in which baseball games are played. Owner includes an employee or agent of the owner.

    3. "Protective seating" means either:

      (a) An area in which a screen to prevent a ball or bat from entering the seating area exists between the spectator and the playing field.

      (b) An area that is reasonably safe for the avoidance of injuries from baseballs, baseball bats or other equipment used by players during a baseball game.

    4. "Spectator" means a person who is present at a

baseball game for the purpose of observing the game, whether or not the person pays an admission fee or is compensated to observe the game.

Although the facts in *Benejam* are unusual, the case is actually typical in many respects. Injured spectators frequently argue that stadium owners and operators have breached the duty of reasonable care by not providing adequate protection against dangers posed by the game. The owners and operators most commonly respond by arguing they have a limited duty that has been met by providing screened areas to protect spectators most at risk. Other owners and operators may argue that the injured spectator assumes certain known risks by attending the game. In either event, batters are not the only ones expected to stay on their toes during a ball game.

Umpire's Ruling

Injuries to Players

Injuries to fans are, thankfully, a rare occurrence at the ballpark. On the other hand, players often suffer minor injuries during a game. Usually, the game proceeds around them until the play is over. For example, a player might pull a hamstring running between bases and get tagged out because he was unable to outrun the fielder.

When an accident "incapacitates" a player or umpire, however, the play should be stopped immediately. Obviously, this rule applies when a player is injured in a way that the umpire believes requires immediate medical attention.

The rule also states that, when the accident prevents a runner from "proceeding to a base to which he is entitled," a substitute runner may advance to the base or bases in place of the injured player.[1] So a batter injured when hit by a pitch need not crawl to first, for example.

Ignorance of this rule led to one of the feel-good sports stories of 2008. Sara Tucholsky, a senior at Western Oregon University, hit the ball over the fence for an apparent home run—the first in the senior's college career—in a softball game against Central Washington University. As she rounded the bases, she suffered a serious knee injury; clearly, this was her final collegiate at-bat. The umpires believed that Tucholsky could be replaced by a pinch runner, but erroneously stated that the runner would be limited to entering at first base with a single, as that was the only base Tucholsky had touched by the time of her injury. They also said that Tucholsky would be called out if her teammates tried to help her around the bases.

Showing a sense of perspective and sportsmanship that one can only hope would obtain above the Division II level at which these colleges play, Tucholsky's opponents from the Central Washington team assisted Tucholsky around the bases. If the umpires had known the rules, we all would have been deprived

of this moving display—perhaps a rare case in which ignorance of the law ended up being a good thing.[2]

1. Rule 5.10(c) and 5.10(c)(1). While there are differences between softball and baseball rules, in this respect they are the same.

2. Graham Hays, *Central Washington offers the ultimate act of sportsmanship*, http://sports.espn.go.com/ncaa/columns/story?id=3372631; Rich Marazzi, *Section 5.10 of rule book allows assistance to base runner*, BASEBALL DIGEST, Sept. 2008, http://findarticles.com/p/articles/mi_m0FCI/is_/ai_n27966088.

The Tenth Inning

Liability for Negligent Medical Assistance to Injured Spectators

Fish v. Los Angeles Dodgers Baseball Club, et al.,
56 Cal. App. 3d 620, 128 Cal. Rptr. 807 (2d Dist. 1976)[1]

When a person is killed because of the wrongful conduct of another person or persons, state law generally provides that a wrongful death action can be brought against those responsible. The details of such actions vary from state to state.

Spectators rarely die from injuries suffered at a baseball game. When this does happen, a wrongful death lawsuit is sure to follow. The *Fish* case examines this situation.

Background Principles of Negligence and Apparent Authority

Negligence claims constitute the vast majority of tort claims litigated today. In order to prevail on a claim of negligence, the

---

1. *Available at* http://login.findlaw.com/scripts/callaw (last visited Sept. 28, 2008). Instructions: Upon linking with this site, you will be required to set up an account. Then you will automatically be taken to the case page.

117

plaintiff must prove that the defendant owed the plaintiff a duty of care. Once that is established, the plaintiff must prove that the defendant breached this duty causing the plaintiff injury. If the plaintiff dies from the injury, the plaintiff's survivors may bring a wrongful death action for the defendant's negligence.

The law of negligence traditionally employs two types of causation—cause-in-fact and cause-in-law. Both types of causation must be met in order to hold a defendant legally accountable.

Cause-in-fact is most commonly established by the plaintiff showing that "but for" the defendant's conduct the harm would have been avoided. A jury is assigned the task of deciding this type of fact-based causation. But establishing cause-in-fact is complicated when separate acts combine to cause the harm or when either act alone would have been sufficient to cause the harm.

In contrast, cause-in-law, which is sometimes confusingly called "proximate cause," is a mechanism used by the law to limit the scope of a defendant's liability. It essentially involves the judicial determination that the defendant should be held legally accountable for the acts causing the harm. The most common approach to deciding proximate cause is the test of "foreseeability." Could the defendant reasonably foresee the harm suffered by the plaintiff?

In some instances, an intervening act by a third person may cause or contribute to the injured person's death. This complicates the analysis but, in general, when two separate acts of negligence combine to cause the death, each actor may be held accountable. In such a case, each person (tortfeasor) is treated as the cause of the death, notwithstanding the fact that only one death occurred.

This result is not, however, inevitable. In some instances, the intervening act by the third person may sever the legal chain of causation to the originally negligent actor. The *Restatement of Torts (Second)* describes this situation as a "superseding cause":

> A superseding cause is an act of a third person or other force which by its intervention prevents the actor from being liable for harm to another which his antecedent negligence is a substantial factor in bringing about.[2]

A superseding cause legally may relieve the original actor from liability, irrespective of whether his or her antecedent negligence was or was not a substantial factor in bringing about the harm. Whether the cause-in-law link is severed is essentially about whether it is morally and practically justified in continuing to hold the original actor liable.

One additional background principle is important before examining *Fish*. When an employer hires an independent contractor, the employer may be held vicariously liable for the contractor's negligence on an apparent or ostensible agency theory. The employer may be held accountable for the appearances that it has created. In short, an employer may be held accountable for the negligent actions of an independent contractor.

The Facts

Alan Fish, a 14-year-old boy, was hit in the head by a line-drive foul ball during a Los Angeles Dodgers night game on May 16. After being struck, Alan slumped forward with his head on his chest and was out like a light for a minute or so. According to the adult companion who was with him at the game but not his parent, Alan then stretched, groaned, and began speaking in an unintelligible fashion. Shortly thereafter, an usher and two ambu-

---

2. Restatement (Second) of Torts § 440 (1965).

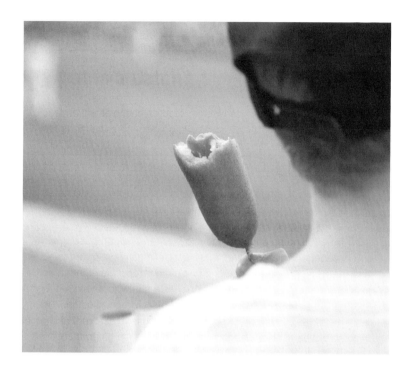

lance attendants arrived at the scene. Alan's condition improved and his speech returned to normal. Notwithstanding this apparent improvement, Alan was taken to the ballpark emergency first-aid station.

Glen E. Jones, M.D., operated the emergency medical facility at the stadium as an independent contractor. He examined Alan's head, took his pulse, looked at his eyes and ears, and tested his reflexes. Dr. Jones did not take Alan's blood pressure or ask about his physical reactions after being hit by the foul ball. Alan remained in the first-aid station for approximately five minutes. He was then told by the doctor that he appeared to be all right and that he could go back to his seat and resume watching the game. Alan was not told to restrict his activities, return to the first-aid station, or see another doctor for follow-up.

Alan watched the remaining six innings of the game without incident. He chased a foul ball, went to the concession stand to buy food, and seemed to have normal speech and physical abilities. On the way out of the stadium, his speech disability returned, and he started to shake and cry. He laid down while he was being driven home by the adult companion. The drive home took approximately 40 minutes.

When Alan arrived home, his parents were told what happened. They took Alan to Citizens Emergency Hospital, where his parents were told that medical attention would not be available for about an hour. Because the boy was pale and limp and appeared to have lost muscular control, his parents drove him to Cedars-Sinai Medical Center. The center told his parents that it could not give him medical attention.

His parents then drove him to Children's Hospital, which was about four blocks from Cedars-Sinai. He was admitted there about midnight, which was about two hours after the Dodgers game ended. He was treated in the emergency clinic at about 1:30 a.m. on May 17. An hour later, at approximately 2:30 a.m. Dr. Johnson, a neurosurgeon, examined the boy and "undertook his care."

At 5 a.m. on May 17, Alan was seen again by Dr. Johnson, who noted the boy was "becoming more alert." Five hours later, at about 10 a.m., Alan's condition had deteriorated, and a cranial angiogram was performed shortly after noon on May 17. The angiogram revealed a "mass" in the boy's brain. Dr. Johnson received permission to do a craniotomy, but this surgery was not performed. On the evening of May 17, at 9:30 p.m., Alan suffered a convulsion that rendered his medical condition terminal. Alan died on May 20 at 1 p.m. when the artificial life support systems to which he was attached were discontinued.

The Lawsuit

The plaintiffs, Alan's parents, sued both the Dodgers and Dr. Jones, the stadium physician.[3] Plaintiffs argued that the doctor was negligent. They argued that he breached his duty of care by not asking whether Alan had been rendered unconscious after being struck, failing to send him in an ambulance for X-rays of his skull, and not limiting Alan's subsequent activities. The plaintiffs also argued that the Dodgers were responsible as the principal for the negligence of their ostensible agent, Dr. Jones.[4]

The testimony of two physicians, who were experts called by the plaintiffs, supported the claim that Dr. Jones had not treated the boy in accordance with the applicable standard of care. One of the experts additionally "suggested, although he did not directly state, that the failure of the staff at Children's Hospital to detect the necessity for and perform emergency surgery, which would have led to survival, was negligent."

The attorney for Dr. Jones argued that his actions were not the legal cause of the boy's death because when the boy arrived at Children's Hospital "it was not too late to save his life by surgery which was indicated by appropriate diagnostic procedures." In short, the hospital's failure to detect the problem and perform the surgery was the cause of the boy's death. Its failure was the superseding cause of the death, and not the actions of Dr. Jones.

The Dodgers' vicarious liability depended on finding Dr. Jones liable. If Dr. Jones was not liable, then the Dodgers were not vicariously liable for his actions. Thus, the success of the

---

3. The two hospitals where Alan was taken after going home from the ballgame were originally named as defendants in the suit, but they were dismissed before the case was submitted to the jury.

4. The plaintiffs also argued that the Dodgers were negligent in failing to provide a safe place for the boy to witness the game, but this claim was dismissed by the trial court before the matter was submitted to the jury.

superseding cause argument was relevant to the liability of both the Dodgers and Dr. Jones.

The attorney for the plaintiffs argued that the jury should be instructed that, legally, there may be more than one cause of death. He argued that the judge should instruct the jury that when the negligent conduct of two or more persons contributes concurrently to the death, the conduct of each of is the legal cause (cause-in-law) of the death regardless of the extent to which each contributes to the death. Therefore, it was no defense that any negligent conduct by Children's Hospital, which was not a party in the litigation, superseded Dr. Jones's negligence.

The court rejected instructing the jury as proposed by the plaintiffs' attorney. It refused to instruct the jury on concurrent causes, superseding causes, and additional harms. Rather, the only jury instruction given by the court was that "a legal cause of a death is a cause which is a substantial factor in bringing about death."

The jury deliberated the case based on whether Dr. Jones's actions or inactions were a "substantial factor" in bringing about Alan's death. It ultimately rendered a verdict in favor of Dr. Jones and the Dodgers.

The Appeal

The plaintiffs appealed to the California Court of Appeal for the Second District. They argued that the trial court, over the plaintiffs' objection, had failed to properly instruct the jury on the law of causation, and that this error resulted in finding no liability. The error, the plaintiffs claimed, also adversely affected their claim against Dodgers.

The plaintiffs argued that Dr. Jones's negligence was a legal cause of Alan's death, and that his negligence converted Alan from a patient who probably would have survived without emergency surgery to a patient whose survival was dependent on emergency surgery. In essence, the hospital's conduct consisted of a failure to protect the boy from the death threatened and caused by the negligence of Dr. Jones. The appellate court reasoned:

> We, therefore, conclude that under the facts of this case, the rule of law applicable rendered irrelevant the existence or degree of the negligence, if any, of the Children's Hospital staff. Under that rule, the claimed negligence of Dr. Jones and the conduct of the Children's Hospital staff were concurrent causes which were operative at the moment of injury. It was no defense to plaintiffs' claim based on Dr. Jones's negligence that the conduct of the Children's Hospital staff was also a substantial factor contributing to decedent's death.

Therefore, the failure of the trial court to give the jury instruction requested by the plaintiffs was erroneous. The judgment in favor of the defendants was reversed and the matter remanded to the trial court. What happened thereafter is not known.

But the general principle of *Fish* is straightforward. Litigants are entitled to jury instructions that fairly and clearly state the essential legal principles applicable to the case. These instructions are legally sufficient when they give a jury a balanced statement of the necessary legal principles applicable to the theories of the case presented. A jury can't make the "call" if it does not have a clear understanding of the ground rules.

Umpire's Ruling

Balls Hitting Players

While a batted or thrown ball can cause
serious injury to fans and players alike, most
contact between horsehide and human just causes discomfort.
How it impacts the game depends on many factors.

A pitched ball that strikes a batter, even on a bounce,
entitles the batter to take first base in most circumstances.
But if the batter does not make an attempt to avoid the ball, the
batter is not entitled to first base. Nor does the batter take first
if the pitch is a strike. That would be true if the batter is hit on
an arm dangling in the strike zone or, more frequently, is hit while
attempting to swing at the ball.

It is sometimes said that the "hands are a part of the bat,"
but if that is true, the batter is holding the bat too tightly. In fact,
the batter is awarded first if hit on the hands as long as contact
occurs outside the strike zone, unless the batter is considered
to have swung at the pitch—not the result that would occur
if the hands really were deemed a part of the bat. If the batter
is swinging or contact occurs in the strike zone, then the call is
"strike" and the ball is dead.[1] It seems that the saying is accurate
when the ball goes foul when glancing off the hands during a
swing, but even here the saying is not technically true—when
the ball hits the batter's hands, it is dead immediately, while a
foul ball is not dead until it is touched or comes to rest in foul
territory.

What if the batter hits the ball and then the ball hits the
batter? If the ball is on or over foul territory, then the ball is
foul unless the batter intentionally "deflects" the ball, in which
case the batter is out.[2] If the ball is fair, however, including being
airborne over fair territory, then the batter is out regardless of
intent, provided that the ball has not first touched a fielder.[3]
Read literally, the rules make no special exception for a batter
struck by a batted ball while still in the batter's box and, since
part of the batter's box is in fair territory, it appears that a batter

Umpire's Ruling (continued)

could be called out for unintentionally touching a ball on or over fair territory even while the batter's feet are still in the box. However, it is common practice for umpires automatically to call the ball "foul" whenever it hits a batter still standing in the box.[4]

If a base runner is struck by a batted ball, the result depends on whether the ball has previously passed an infielder. If it has not, the runner is out;[5] if it has passed an infielder and touches the runner "immediately behind" the fielder, or if the ball has been deflected by a fielder, the ball is in play unless the umpire determines that another infielder could have made a play on the ball, in which case interference is called and the runner is out. The runner is also out even if no other infielder could have made a play on the ball if the umpire concludes that the runner "deliberately and intentionally kicks" the ball.[6]

---

1. Rule 6.08(b).
2. Rule 6.05(i).
3. Rule 6.05(g).
4. RICK RODER, MORE THAN 100 PROBLEMS WITH THE OFFICIAL BASEBALL RULES 52 (2007).
5. Rule 7.08(f).
6. Rule 7.09(k).

Former MLB Players Argue Reverse Discrimination

Moran v. Selig, 447 F.3d 748 (9th Cir. 2006)[1]

Prior to 1947, African-Americans were banned from playing major league baseball (MLB). Banned baseball players were limited to playing in the "Negro leagues," which were professional baseball teams composed exclusively of black baseball players. After Jackie Robinson broke the color barrier in 1947, the Negro leagues eventually faded away as MLB became integrated. But the history of discrimination was not forgotten.

MLB voluntarily decided in the 1990s to provide medical and supplemental income benefits to eligible former Negro league players. Whether the benefit plans were to remedy this history of past discrimination against African-Americans or simply forward looking acts of charitable kindness, the result was the same: The MLB special benefit plans were made available only to those blacks who played baseball in the Negro leagues.

---

1. *Available at* http://www.ca9.uscourts.gov/ca9/newopinions.nsf/A19E2EB47F95 923E8825716800 7c9290/$file/0455647.pdf?openelement (last visited Sept. 28, 2008).

One MLB benefit plan was called the Negro League Medical Plan, which was adopted in 1993. The other was the Negro League Supplemental Income Plan, which was adopted four years later in 1997. The income plan required an eligible African-American player to have played at least one season in the Negro leagues prior to 1948, and a total of four seasons of professional baseball in the Negro leagues, major leagues, or both. Eligible black players could receive an annual payment of $10,000.

Many players qualifying for the special benefit plans played MLB from 1947 to 1979. Under the then-existing MLB pension and medical benefit plans, they were disqualified from eligibility because they failed to play long enough in the majors to vest. But the special plan allowed those black players to "tack" their playing service in the Negro leagues with their MLB service to qualify for benefits.

The Claim of Reverse Discrimination

Mike Colbern, a Caucasian who played for the Chicago White Sox in 1978 and 1979, was ineligible for a pension or medical benefits under MLB's then existing "four-season" rule. Following the baseball strike of 1981, this "four-season" eligibility rule was changed to allow a MLB player to become vested for medical benefits after one day and for pension benefits after 43 days. But this change in the vesting rule did not apply to players whose careers ended prior to 1980, which was Mike's problem. He was caught in a benefit "squeeze play."

In 2003, Mike and similarly situated ineligible former MLB players, including Richard Alan Moran,[2] filed a complaint with

---

2. The name Moran appears in the abbreviated title to the case. It refers to Richard Alan Moran, who played for the New York Mets in 1963 and 1964. Mike Colbern and other players were also plaintiffs.

the Equal Employment Opportunity Commission (EEOC), which is responsible for enforcing various federal laws that prohibit discrimination in employment. The EEOC enforces, among other federal laws, Title VII of the Civil Rights Act of 1964. Among other things, Title VII prohibits employment discrimination based on race.

Mike and his colleagues claimed that MLB had arbitrarily, intentionally, and unlawfully excluded them from the Negro League Plans on the basis of race. If the former Negro League players were able to enjoy special employment benefits, then Title VII gives them the same participation opportunity. The EEOC responded by issuing them a "right-to-sue" letter, which effectively opened the door for suing in federal district court.

Plaintiffs brought a class action[3] for discrimination, as well as other actions,[4] in the U.S. District Court for the Central District of California.[5] The named defendants included Commissioner Allan H. "Bud" Selig, MLB, and individually named MLB clubs.

The plaintiffs were ineligible for MLB pension or medical benefits because they had not played long enough to satisfy the vesting requirements. Some of the plaintiffs missed qualifying by a matter of days. Others would have received both a pension and

---

3. The Federal Rules of Civil Procedure govern class actions. Rule 23 provides that the class action must have certain characteristics, including (1) the class must be so large that individual suits would be impractical; (2) there must be legal or factual claims in common to the class; (3) the claims or defenses must be typical of the plaintiffs or defendants; and (4) the representative parties must fairly and adequately protect the interests of the class.

4. Plaintiffs, during their participation in MLB, allegedly received systematic injections of cortisone and other drugs in dangerous amounts. MLB team trainers and doctors failed to inform plaintiffs of the known risks associated with these drugs. These alleged facts were the principal basis of their claims of negligence and intentional battery against the defendants.

5. Ninety-nine percent of the plaintiffs were Caucasians who played Major League baseball from 1947 to 1979. The remaining 1 percent were Latino.

medical benefits under the vesting requirements employed by MLB after 1980. Many of the plaintiffs were destitute and could not afford the medical care necessitated by their playing in the majors.

The district court granted the defendants summary judgment. It determined no issues of material fact were in dispute and that the defendants were entitled to a judgment as a matter of law. The effect of the court's decision was to give MLB the right to exclude more than 1,000 former players from a pension and medical benefit plans available solely for qualifying former Negro League players.

To survive summary judgment on their Title VII claim of disparate treatment, plaintiffs had to show 1) that they belonged to a protected class; 2) they were qualified for their jobs; 3) they were subjected to an adverse employment action; and 4) similarly situated employees not in their protected class received more favorable treatment. The plaintiffs met the first two criteria, so the principal focus was on requirements (3) and (4).

The overarching principle advanced by the plaintiffs was that the Civil Rights Act of 1964 protects everyone, without regard to race, from employment discrimination because of race. This core idea has been affirmed by the U.S. Supreme Court:

> Title VII of the Civil Rights Act of 1964 prohibits the discharge of "any individual" because of "such individual's race." Its terms are not limited to discrimination against members of any particular race . . . . We therefore hold today that Title VII prohibits racial discrimination against the white petitioners in this case upon the same standards as would be applicable were they Negroes and Jackson white.[6]

The plaintiffs appealed the district court's decision to the Ninth Circuit Court of Appeals, which affirmed the trial court. Why did the plaintiffs strike out? The Ninth Circuit gave several reasons.

First, it found that the plaintiffs were not subject to an adverse employment action. Disparate treatment of a voluntary benefit program may constitute a claim under Title VII, but only when the benefits are awarded on the basis of an "employment relationship."

Eligibility was based on being a former Negro League player. The benefit was not an incident of employment by MLB. The court reasoned that the benefits were based on an employment relationship with a legal entity, a Negro League team that was legally distinct from MLB. Therefore, the fact that the plaintiffs did not receive the same or substantially similar benefits could not be considered an "adverse employment action" by MLB.

The second reason focused on the characteristics of the two

---

6. McDonald v. Santa Fe Trail Transp. Co., 427 U.S. 278, 280 (1976).

classes of players. In order to show that one class of "employees" received more favorable treatment, the classes must be "similarly situated in all material respects."

The court states:

> Although there are indeed some similarities between [plaintiffs'] circumstances and that of the players to whom they compare themselves, the two groups are not similar in "all material respects." Unlike the beneficiaries of the Negro League Plans, [plaintiffs] were never prevented from playing for a MLB team, and thus unable to acquire the necessary longevity, for reasons entirely independent of their ability to do the job (i.e., on account of their race). Nor did [plaintiffs] ever play in the Negro Leagues, a primary requirement for eligibility under the Negro League Plans.

The plaintiffs were not banned from playing in MLB. In contrast, MLB's absolute ban on black players before 1947 did prevent those players from accumulating the necessary years of service to qualify for benefits.

Moreover, rather than being disadvantaged, some of the plaintiffs may have been advantaged by the pre-1947 exclusion. The ban on blacks meant that fewer players competed for roster spots on MLB clubs, which arguably made it easier to qualify for the benefit plan then in effect.

Finally, the court offered an alternate rationale for rejecting the plaintiffs' claim. Assuming that a plaintiff establishes a prima facie case of discrimination under Title VII, which the court found the plaintiffs had failed to do, the judicial inquiry does not end. Rather the "burden of proof" shifts to the defendant-employer to show that a legitimate, non-discriminatory reason exists for the disparate treatment. If the defendant-employer offers such evidence, the plaintiff-employee may offer evidence to rebut this evidence. The plaintiff-employee ultimately may prevail by proving the defendant-employer's justification is simply a disguised pretext for discrimination.

The court reasoned that MLB had shown a legitimate, nondiscriminatory reason for its decision to provide benefits to former Negro League players. It was not, in the court's view, pretextual in any respect or rebutted by the plaintiffs. Summary judgment was appropriate because any prima facie case that might have been established by the plaintiffs was adequately rebutted by MLB's justification for the disparate treatment.

A Loss is a Loss

In the 1888 poem, "Casey at the Bat," by Ernest Thayer, a baseball team from the fictional town of Mudville is losing by two runs with two outs in the bottom of the ninth. Two men are on base. The "mighty Casey" is at bat. He takes two strikes without swinging. The game is on the line: "And now the air is shattered by the force of Casey's blow . . . But there is no joy in Mudville— mighty Casey has struck out." Undoubtedly, Mike Colbern and his colleagues know the feeling.

Umpire's Ruling

Two Wrongs Make a Right

So-called "reverse discrimination," as alleged in the *Moran* case, is illegal unless it is a remedy for past discrimination. The idea that two wrongs can make a right also appears in the Rules of Baseball.

When a pitcher begins the delivery to the plate with a runner on base, the pitcher must complete the delivery or be called for a balk. But in the major leagues, if the batter steps out the batter's box without permission after the pitcher begins the delivery, the pitcher can stop without penalty. According to the rules, "both the pitcher and batter have violated a rule and the umpire shall call time and both the batter and pitcher start over from 'scratch.'"[1]

A similar situation occurs when a batter hits out of order. The umpire does not call the violation unless the defensive team appeals. If the improper batter concludes the time at bat and a pitch is thrown to the next batter, the improper batter becomes a proper batter, and the next legal batter is whoever's name follows the "legalized improper batter," regardless of who would have been the proper batter in the absence of the mistake.

---

1. Comment to Rule 6.02(b) for Major League Play only.

To Breach or Not to Breach: That Is the Question[1]

ESPN, Inc. v. Office of the Commissioner of Baseball,
76 F. Supp. 2d 383 (S.D.N.Y. 1999)[2]

Major league baseball (MLB) is in business to make money and, by most accounts, it is doing a good job of it. In 2007, for example, the commissioner of baseball, Allan H. (Bud) Selig, said revenues were more than $6 billion. Notwithstanding a well-publicized set of concerns, the commissioner predicts continued economic growth for the "nation's pastime."

The broadcast media contributes a significant amount of lucre to baseball's revenue stream. Over the years, MLB has had a series of revenue-producing relationships with different broadcast partners, including CBS, ABC, NBC, Fox Broadcasting Company, Time Warner's TBS, DirecTV, cable systems, and various satellite providers. Baseball's broadcast contract with

---

1. *See* William Shakespeare, *Hamlet*, Act III, Scene I:

   To be, or not to be, that is the Question:
   Whether 'tis Nobler in the minde to suffer
   The Slings and Arrowes of outragious Fortune,
   Or to take Armes against a Sea of troubles . . .

2. *Available at* http://www.law.unlv.edu/faculty/bam/k2001/briefs/espn-1.html (last visited Sept. 28, 2008).

ESPN turned sour and wound up in court. But as baseball fans know, ESPN and MLB are still in a committed economic relationship.

In 1999, the all-sports cable television network ESPN sued the Office of Major League Baseball, which acts on behalf of the MLB clubs, for money damages and for declaratory and injunctive relief in the U.S. District Court for the Southern District of New York. ESPN argued that MLB refused to honor its telecast contract. In response, MLB argued that it had the right to immediately terminate the contract even though several additional years were left on the contract.[3] It argued that ESPN had breached its part of the bargain.

Before the case went to trial, the parties filed numerous motions in limine.[4] These pre-trial motions ask the judge to rule as a matter of law that certain evidence and arguments be found to be admissible or inadmissible at trial. In *ESPN, Inc. v. Office of the Commissioner of Baseball*, the court ruled on these motions.

The Contract

To understand the disagreement, one must begin with the language of the contract. In 1996, the parties signed a contract that gave ESPN the right to telecast regular season major league games. In return, ESPN agreed to pay yearly fees and to produce baseball telecasts on Wednesday and Sunday nights during the

---

3. The original contract term was Jan. 1, 1996, through Nov. 1, 2000, or the last game of the 2000 World Series. The contract was amended, extending the term through the last game of the 2002 World Series, or Nov. 1, 2002.

4. Ten separate motions in limine were filed by the parties. ESPN's motion in limine dealing with MLB's damages is reported separately at *ESPN, Inc. v. Comm'r of Baseball*, 76 F. Supp. 2d 416 (S.D.N.Y. 1999) (holding that MLB could not recover damages for loss of profits, damage to reputation, or loss of goodwill; it could recover nominal damages; and finally, that it could introduce evidence of material breach by ESPN, even though it was not entitled to anything other than nominal damages).

regular baseball season. As might be expected, the written contract spelled out in more detail the respective rights and duties of the parties.

The contract contained several provisions central to deciding the motions in limine. The first was the promise by ESPN that "it has not made nor will make any contractual or other commitments that conflict with or will prevent full performance" of the contract. This provision became the flashpoint for the controversy when ESPN unilaterally substituted NFL football games for MLB baseball games.

The second important contract provision gave ESPN the right to preempt up to 10 baseball games a season with baseball's prior written approval. This clause also provided that approval could not be unreasonably withheld.

The parties used the following language to express this understanding:

> With the prior written approval of Baseball, which shall not be unreasonably withheld or delayed, ESPN may . . . preempt any [Baseball game telecast] hereunder, up to a maximum of ten [Baseball game telecasts] per year, for an event of significant viewer interest.

The contract also allowed ESPN to telecast the preempted baseball games on ESPN's secondary cable service, ESPN2.

The final important provision was the "no-waiver" clause. Essentially, this type of clause provides that the failure of a party to act does not constitute a waiver of its rights. Such clauses are used in contracts to prevent the inadvertent waiver of rights by a party by requiring that any waiver of a right be in writing to avoid hidden ball tricks.

The no-waiver clause used in the ESPN-MLB contract stated:

The failure of either party to seek redress for any violation of, or to insist upon the strict performance of, any term of this Agreement shall not constitute a waiver of such rights or in any way limit or prevent the subsequent enforcement of any such term. All waivers must be made in writing. Any waiver of a right or remedy pertaining to this Agreement shall not be deemed to be a waiver of any other right or remedy. The various rights and remedies of either party contained herein shall not be considered exclusive of, but shall be considered cumulative to, any rights or remedies now or hereafter existing at law, in equity or by statute or regulation.

The Facts

Before their disagreement boiled over into litigation, MLB had, over the years, granted ESPN's requests for preemption in all 15 prior instances when requested.[5] But in the late 1990s, MLB started playing hardball with ESPN.

In January 1998, ESPN asked MLB to approve the telecast of three NFL games in place of three baseball games. MLB refused to give prior written approval for ESPN to preempt the games. Without receiving baseball's prior written approval, ESPN went ahead and substituted the NFL games anyway. But MLB then refused to allow ESPN to show the preempted games on ESPN2. Things were heating up.

In January 1999, the same series of events occurred. ESPN asked to preempt three baseball games for NFL games, MLB

---

5. According to ESPN's complaint, MLB previously had approved, pursuant to the "significant viewer interest" waiver clause, requests that included, e.g., the Senior U.S. Open, the U.S. Open, the College World Series, and early-round NHL playoff games. It also alleged that each of the NFL games that preempted a baseball game was "an event of significant viewer interest."

refused, and ESPN went ahead and preempted the baseball games for the football games without receiving written approval. MLB again refused to allow ESPN to show the preempted baseball games on ESPN2. At this point, if not before, it was clear that the parties were headed for a legal showdown. The kabuki dance could not continue.

Why did MLB refuse ESPN's preemption requests? The answer depends on one's view. According to ESPN, MLB was attempting "to extort hundreds of millions of dollars of economic concessions as the 'price' for its consent." Arguably, MLB was using the consent clause as leverage to renegotiate their deal so as to get more money from ESPN. In short, it was all about wringing more money out of the network. From MLB's perspective, the refusal was about not continuing to take a back seat to football. The pride of the "national pastime" was at stake.

ESPN's seeming insouciance in acting without written consent is puzzling. If ESPN thought MLB was acting unreasonably, it should have sought judicial intervention to determine this fact. Its failure to do so leads one to wonder whether it feared an adverse legal ruling, which may have led to the loss of millions of dollars in revenues. Regardless of its motive, ESPN engaged in "self-help" by preempting the baseball games without written permission.

Election of Remedies

In April 1999, MLB sent a letter notifying ESPN that it "hereby terminates the Agreement." In analyzing the legal arguments, the court separated the 1998 and 1999 events. The court concluded that MLB had no right to terminate the contract based on ESPN's alleged material breaches occurring in 1998. It had the right to damages for any proven breach, but it could not terminate the contract.

But what about the clause that required waivers to be in writing? ESPN did not have written permission to preempt their games. Was that not a material breach triggering the right to terminate?

The court found that MLB lost its right to terminate the contract based on the events surrounding in 1998 breach. It might be able to get damages for the breach, but it could not terminate the contract. The court reasoned that the events occurring in 1998 were controlled by the doctrine of election of remedies. This doctrine requires that a non-breaching party, in this case MLB, upon learning of a material breach, must choose between terminating the contract and claiming damages for total breach, or continuing the contract and claiming damages for partial breach. The options are mutually exclusive.

The evidence revealed that MLB elected to continue the contract beyond 1998 and into 1999. Thus, it could not thereafter change its mind and terminate the contract based on the alleged breaches occurring in 1998. The court found that the election to continue the contract was the exercise of its right, and not the waiver of its rights. Therefore, the no-waiver clause, which required written permission, did not provide a basis for ruling that MLB could terminate the contract.

The court refused to consider whether the parties could theoretically contract around the election of remedies doctrine because there was no evidence that the parties had attempted to do so in the 1996 contract. Because the agreement did not purport to contractually limit the application of election of remedies, this question was not properly before the court. In other words, its application would have no bearing on the outcome.

Although MLB was barred from terminating the contract based on the alleged 1998 breach, MLB also sought to terminate the contract based on ESPN's preemption in 1999. Predictably,

ESPN argued that the election doctrine also applied because MLB elected to continue the contract for the remainder of the 1999 season after it sent the April 21, 1999, termination letter. MLB, it argued, had received the full fee of $3.4 million from ESPN for the broadcast of more than 80 baseball games during the entire season. In short, MLB continued to accept performance from ESPN for nearly six additional months after it purported to terminate the contract. Therefore, according to ESPN, MLB was pursing two inconsistent remedies, which the election of remedies doctrine precludes.

But this time the court found that MLB did not elect to pursue inconsistent remedies. Baseball notified ESPN that it would accept no "new" performance after the conclusion of the 1999 season. The court reasoned that MLB's letter dated April 21, 1999, to ESPN gave "present notice of future termination" without running afoul of the election of remedies doctrine.

From an economic as well as legal perspective, the court's reasoning made considerable practical sense given the seasonal nature of baseball. Games and programs are set well in advance, and relied on by the parties as well as non-parties to the contract, including advertisers, the media, and the fans. Demanding contract termination in April, or during mid-performance by the parties, would exact too high a cost to all concerned.

Self-Help, Called Out

According to ESPN, MLB unreasonably withheld its preemption request, and this entitled ESPN to treat the refusal as a "nullity." In other words, it had the right to ignore the refusal and to proceed as though the request had been granted. This theory, ESPN argued, allowed it to engage in "self-help" by broadcasting the NFL games without written approval. In the spirit of generosity,

ESPN conceded, however, that if MLB's refusal was found reasonable then the theory of self-help was unavailable.

The court rejected ESPN's argument. Most cases approving the use of self-help, at least when it is not expressly and knowingly agreed to by the parties, involve cases where a landlord has unreasonably withheld a tenant's request to sublease an apartment to a subtenant. The legal principle is based on the real property principle that disfavors restrictions on the free transfer of land because it tends to prevent the full utilization of the land.[6]

The same policy was not at work here. The court concluded ESPN could not claim a breach, invoke the principle of self-help, and only perform those obligations it wished to perform. If a contract is breached, the non-breaching party has two options. It can terminate the agreement and sue for total breach or it can continue the contract and sue for partial breach. Consequently, the court refused to extend the principle of self-help to commercial contracts. Undoubtedly, it would have been a more difficult case for the court had the parties contractually agreed to the remedy of self-help, but they had not.

The Final Score

The holdings of the court may be summarized. First, the "no waiver" clause did not permit the termination of the 1996 contract based on ESPN's alleged material breach by preempting certain baseball telecasts. Second, if ESPN's preemption constituted a material breach, baseball did not act inconsistently with its termination option by waiting until after the end of the 1999

---

6. Historically, the common law allowed a landlord to use self-help to retake leased premises from a tenant in possession without incurring liability, provided the landlord was entitled to possession and did so peacefully. Today, most jurisdictions require landlords to use the judicial process to recover possession in such cases.

baseball season to terminate the contract. The April notice was not controlling. Finally, assuming MLB unreasonably withheld its approval of ESPN's preemption requests, ESPN did not have the right to resort to "self-help" by preempting the baseball telecasts. It should have gone to court to resolve the matter of unreasonableness.

A Final Thought

The technological platforms for delivering baseball games to fans will continue to evolve to satisfy consumer demand. Live broadcast, delayed delivery, and on-demand viewing across the digital spectrum will be part of the entertainment mix. Cable and satellite delivery systems will continue to be important delivery platforms.

In 2009, MLB plans to expand its delivery of baseball programming when it launches the MLB Network. This network will broadcast baseball programming 24 hours a day, seven days a week on a year-round basis. From a historical perspective, this network is just another step in the evolution of delivering and controlling baseball viewing.[7] Like the batter with three balls and no strikes, MLB is in the "catbird seat."[8]

7. *See* Pittsburgh Athletic Co. v. KQV Broadcasting Co., 24 F. Supp. 490 (W.D. Pa. 1938) (holding that baseball clubs have the exclusive right to control the broadcast of their games and are protected from unauthorized broadcasts by the law of unfair competition).

8. The term "catbird seat" was used by James Thurber in his 1942 humorous short story "The Catbird Seat." Red Barber, the legendary baseball broadcaster and Thurber fan, popularized its use in the world of baseball.

Umpire's Ruling

Election of Remedies

While the party to a contract, as in the *ESPN* case, might get to choose the remedy for a contract violation, the wronged party in a baseball game usually doesn't get to choose the remedy. But that isn't always true.

Catcher's interference usually occurs when a catcher sets up too close to the batter, the batter swings, and the bat clips the catcher's glove. The manager of the offensive team may elect to have the batter take first base. But suppose that, after making contact with the catcher's glove, the batter strikes a weak grounder, scoring a runner from third while the batter is thrown out at first base. The offensive team may keep the result of the play.[1] A similar election is permitted when the pitcher commits a balk—for instance, if while pitching from the stretch with a runner on base, the pitcher fails to come to an adequate stop before throwing home. The offensive manager may elect to take the result of the play.[2]

---

1. Rule 6.09 provides:

If a play follows the interference, the manager of the offense may advise the plate umpire that he elects to decline the interference penalty and accept the play. Such election shall be made immediately at the end of the play. However, if the batter reaches first base on a hit, an error, a base on balls, a hit batsman, or otherwise, and all other runners advance at least one base, the play proceeds without reference to the interference.

2. Rule 8.02b provides:

If a play follows the violation called by the umpire, the manager of the team at bat may advise the umpire-in-chief that he elects to accept the play. Such election shall be made immediately at the end of the play. However, if the batter reaches first base on a hit, an error, a base on balls, a hit batsman, or otherwise, and no other runner is put out before advancing at least one base, the play shall proceed without reference to the violation.

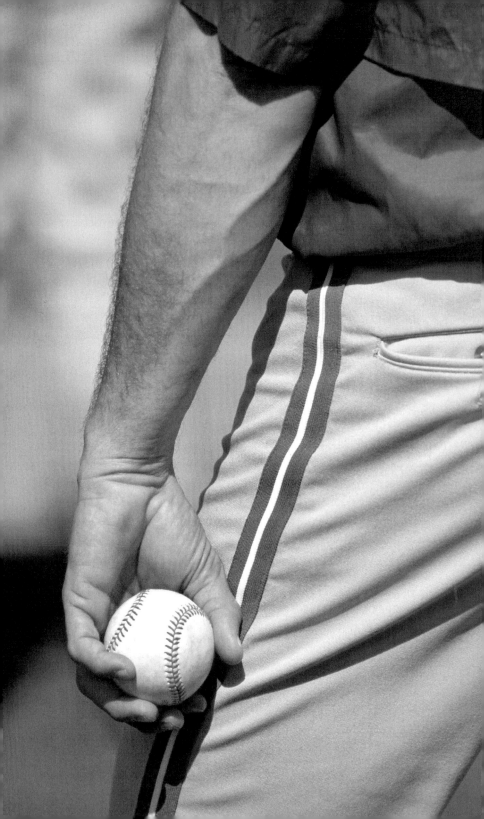

Pitcher Safety and Metal Bats

Sanchez v. Hillerich & Bradsby Co.,
104 Cal. App. 4th 703 (2002)[1]

laying the game of baseball involves some inherent risks.[2] One risk for a defensive player is getting hit by a batted ball. Notwithstanding Yogi Berra's claim that "all pitchers are liars and crybabies," the pitcher is in an especially vulnerable position. In 2003, for example, an 18-year-old American Legion pitcher was killed when a batter using a metal bat hit a line drive

---

1. *Available at* http://login.findlaw.com/scripts/callaw?dest=ca/caapp4th/104/703.html (last visited Sept. 28, 2008). Instructions: Upon linking with this site, you will be required to set up an account. Then you will automatically be taken to the case page.

2. As previously discussed in *Fish v. Los Angeles Dodgers Baseball Club*, spectators also are exposed to certain risks during a game.

Umpires are exposed to risk. In June 2008, for example, plate umpire Brian O'Nora was hit in the head by the sheared-off barrel of a maple bat during an MLB game between the Kansas City Royals and the Colorado Rockies. O'Nora was taken to the hospital, where he remained overnight. Some argue that maple bats, which are preferred by many MLB players, splinter with greater force than those made of ash. Commissioner Bud Selig has said that shattering maple bats are "a source of concern for me."

Base coaches also are at risk. Mike Coolbaugh was in his first season as the hitting coach for the Tulsa Drillers, the Colorado Rockies Double-A affiliate, when he was struck in the neck by a foul ball while coaching first base on July 22, 2007. The ball, which is estimated to have been traveling over 100 mph, instantly killed him. MLB responded to his death by adopting a new rule in November 2007. Major and minor league base coaches must now wear helmets when they are on the field.

back at him, striking him in the temple.[3] Death or severe injuries from being struck by batted balls are rare. They do, however, happen.

The debate over the use of non-wood bats in baseball and the risks associated with their use has been going on for at least 20 years. The controversy continues unabated today. The rules of major league baseball (MLB) require the use of solid wood bats in the majors.[4] Although the majors prohibit the use of non-wood bats, metal bats were introduced in the 1970s as a cost-saving alternative to wood bats that were prone to break. The National Sporting Goods Association reports that the sale of wood bats makes up a small percentage in the bat industry. In 2006, it reported that consumers spent about $147 million on 2.3 million metal composite bats.

The familiar "ping" made by a batter using an aluminum, titanium, or other metal bat during little league, Babe Ruth, high

---

3. *Available at* http://www.billingsgazette.net/articles/2003/07/27/sports/export 115285.txt (last visited June 28, 2008).

4. MLB Official Rules, Section 1.10:

(a) The bat shall be a smooth, round stick not more than 2-3/4 inches in diameter at the thickest part and not more than 42 inches in length. The bat shall be one piece of solid wood. NOTE: No laminated or experimental bats shall be used in a professional game (either championship season or exhibition games) until the manufacturer has secured approval from the Rules Committee of his design and methods of manufacture.

(b) Cupped Bats. An indentation in the end of the bat up to one inch in depth is permitted and may be no wider than two inches and no less than one inch in diameter. The indentation must be curved with no foreign substance added.

(c) The bat handle, for not more than 18 inches from its end, may be covered or treated with any material or substance to improve the grip. Any such material or substance, which extends past the 18 inch limitation, shall cause the bat to be removed from the game. NOTE: If the umpire discovers that the bat does not conform to (c) above until a time during or after which the bat has been used in play, it shall not be grounds for declaring the batter out, or ejected from the game.

(d) No colored bat may be used in a professional game unless approved by the Rules Committee.

Although MLB only allows bats made from solid wood in its games, it allows the use of composite bats that it has evaluated and approved as comparable to "one-piece solid northern white ash bats" in the minor league short-season.

school, and college baseball games is a testament to their widespread use outside of professional baseball. Metal bats are popular for several reasons. Metal bats, which are more durable and thus have a longer life than wood bats, typically have a higher performance level than wood bats. They produce a "trampoline effect," have a larger "sweet spot"[5] and are lighter than wood bats. Notwithstanding the fact that the speed of the pitch and the strength of the batter are important independent variables in measuring the exit speed of the ball from the bat, the performance factors associated with the metal bat generally translate into a greater hit-ball velocity.

Although an increased hit-ball velocity is advantageous for the batter, it arguably places the defensive player, especially the pitcher, at a disadvantage by having less time to react to a "come-back" ball. The distance between home plate and the pitcher's mound on a regulation baseball field is 60 feet 6 inches. Immediately after the pitcher releases the ball, the actual distance between the pitcher and the batter will be significantly less because the pitcher's momentum carries the pitcher toward the batter.

A ball traveling at a speed of 97 miles per hour (mph) will reach the pitcher in about .4 of a second. According to a batting-cage empirical study comparing the performance of metal and wood bats reported in *Medicine & Science in Sports and Exercise*, almost 40 percent of the well-struck baseballs hit with a metal bat typically traveled at speeds of more than 100 mph.[6] A ball traveling at 110 mph allows a college pitcher, according to some calculations, sufficient time to avoid being hit. For com-

---

5. One 2001 sports journal study reported that the "sweet spot" of an aluminum bat may be 470 percent larger than that of a comparable wood bat.

6. Joseph J. Crisco et al., *Batting Performance of Wood and Metal Baseball Bats*, 34 MED. & SCI. IN SPORTS & EXERCISE 1675, 1678 (2002).

Federal Register / Vol. 65, No. 116 / Thursday, June 15, 2000 / Notices   37525

CONSUMER PRODUCT SAFETY COMMISSION

Petition Requesting Performance Requirments for Non-Wood Baseball Bats

AGENCY: Consumer Product Safety Commission.
ACTION: Notice.

SUMMARY: The Commission has received a petition (CP 00–1) requesting that the Commission issue a performance standard for non-wood baseball bats. The Commission solicits written comments concerning the petition.

DATES: The Office of the Secretary must receive comments on the petition by August 14, 2000.

ADDRESSES: Comments, preferably in five copies, on the petition should be mailed to the Office of the Secretary, Consumer Product Safety Commission, Washington, DC 20207, telephone (301) 504–0800, or delivered to the Office of the Secretary, Room 501, 4330 East-West Highway, Bethesda, Maryland 20814. Comments may also be filed by telefacsimile to (301) 504–0127 or by email to cpsc-os@cpsc.gov. Comments should be captioned "Petition CP 00–1, Petition on Baseball Bats." A copy of the petition is available for inspection at the Commission's Public Reading Room, Room 419, 4330 East-West Highway, Bethesda, Maryland.

FOR FURTHER INFORMATION CONTACT: Rockelle Hammond, Office of the Secretary, Consumer Product Safety Commission, Washington, D.C. 20207; telephone (301) 504–0800, ext. 1232.

SUPPLEMENTARY INFORMATION: The Commission has received correspondence from J.W. MacKay, Jr. requesting that the Commission issue a rule requiring that all non-wood baseball bats perform like wood bats. The Commission is docketing his request as a petition under the Consumer Product Safety Act. 15 U.S.C. 2056 and 2058. The petitioner asserts that non-wood bats (primarily made of aluminum and composite materials) have become increasingly dangerous. He states that such bats have a faster bat swing speed, a larger "sweet spot," and lower balance point than wood bats. These high performance bats, he asserts, allow the ball to achieve a faster exit velocity so that the pitcher does not have time to react if a ball is batted at him. For these reasons, the petitioner argues, such non-wood bats present an unreasonable risk of injury.

Interested parties may obtain a copy of the petition by writing or calling the Office of the Secretary, Consumer Product Safety Commission, Washington, DC 20207; telephone (301) 504–0800. Copies of the petition are also available for inspection from 8:30 a.m. to 5 p.m., Monday through Friday, in the Commission's Public Reading Room, Room 419, 4330 East-West Highway, Bethesda, Maryland.

Dated: June 9, 2000.

Sadye E. Dunn,
Secretary, Consumer Product Safety Commission.
[FR Doc. 00–15062 Filed 6–14–00; 8:45 am]
BILLING CODE 6355±01±P

parison purposes, a ball must leave a bat at a minimum speed of 110 mph to clear the fence in most MLB parks.

Ultimately, the speed of the ball may not be as significant as the time available for the pitcher to react to the come-back ball. It is the reaction time a pitcher has to deal with a line drive that is important. The reaction time is affected by the pitcher's style of delivery. The delivery may leave the pitcher in an awkward fielding position. Although pitchers are typically coached on the proper follow-through, the pitcher is always at risk of being hit regardless of whether a metal or wood bat is used. If the pitcher is out of position to field the come-back ball, the risk of being hit is increased. According to one expert, a properly positioned college pitcher should be able to deflect or avoid a ball traveling at a speed of up to 120 mph.

Although metal composite bats are prohibited in the majors, MLB pitchers are not immune from injury from come-back line drives from wood bats. In 1957, for example, Herb Score, the young "ace pitcher" for the Cleveland Indians, was hit in the eye by a line drive hit by Gil McDougald, a renowned infielder for the New York Yankees. The injury ended his season. Although Herb made a partial comeback in 1958 and pitched a full season in 1959, he was never the same quality pitcher due to the injury.

More recently, in 2008, Chris Young, the starting pitcher for the San Diego Padres, was hit in the face by a hard-hit line drive by Albert Pujols, who was batting for the St. Louis Cardinals. Young suffered a nasal fracture and lacerations from the line drive. Although Chris was disabled for a time, the injury did not end his season like it did Herb Score's.

On to the Courts

In some instances, the battle over the use of metal bats has shifted to the courts. In 1999, Andrew Sanchez was pitching for California State University, Northridge (CSUN). During the game, he was hit in the head by a come-back line drive ball. Andrew suffered severe head injuries, including a fractured skull. The ball was hit by Dominic Correa who was using an aluminum bat. At the time of the accident, Dominic was playing baseball for the University of Southern California (USC), which is a member of the Pac-10 athletic conference.

Although Andrew was flattened, he did not take the injury lying down. In 2000, he filed suit in California Superior Court against Hillerich & Bradsby Company (H&B) (the bat manufacturer), USC (which provided the bat), the National Collegiate Athletic Association (which allowed metal bats), and the Pac-10. He claimed the defendants were both negligent and accountable under products liability law for allowing the use of a dangerous bat that substantially increased the risk of his being injured.

H&B was an obvious party to the litigation because it designed and manufactured the "Air Attack 2" aluminum bat used by Dominic. The bat was a hollow aluminum alloy design with a pressurized air bladder. H&B employees were instructed to make bats that conformed to the regulations of the "various regulatory bodies involved." According to the bat designer, who was an employee of H&B at the time, the bat was expressly designed to increase the speed of the ball as it leaves the barrel of the bat.

The National Collegiate Athletic Association (NCAA) was sued because its rules govern baseball bats used in athletic events, including those played in the Pac-10. The bat used by Dominic "apparently" had been approved by the NCAA.[7] Moreover, the NCAA was aware of the danger because it had notified the athletic conferences, including the Pac-10, of the dangerous nature of newer metal bats and of its decision to implement new rules on the maximum batted ball exit velocity and new size and weight specifications for non-wood bats.

USC had an agreement with H&B that provided USC would be compensated for exclusively using H&B's bats. That agreement and providing the bat to Dominic was the basis for USC

---

7. "At the time of the accident, the NCAA allowed the use of metal bats, and the bat in use was *apparently* in compliance with NCAA standards." Sanchez v. Hillerich & Bradsby Co., 128 Cal. Rptr. 2d 529, 536 (Ct. App. 2002).

being named a defendant. The Pac-10 presumably was named because it had been notified of the dangerous nature of the newer metal bats.[8]

The Superior Court Proceeding

The defendants individually filed motions for summary judgment. H&B argued that the plaintiff could not establish legal causation, that the doctrine of primary assumption of the risk foreclosed liability, and that the bat complied with the rules promulgated by the NCAA. The assumption of the risk argument was based on the claim that one of the inherent risks that a pitcher assumes in playing the game is being hit by a come-back ball. It also argued that Andrew had signed a waiver or disclaimer form acknowledging the risk of playing on the team and consenting to the risk of injury at the beginning of the season.

The NCAA argued it did not owe Andrew a duty "because at the time of the accident the baseball community was in significant disagreement over the risk of aluminum bats." It also argued primary assumption of the risk and the lack of legal causation. USC and the Pac-10 based their motion on the primary assumption of the risk doctrine.

The plaintiff opposed the motions. He offered testimony by the designer of the Air Attack 2 model, Jack Mackay. Mackay testified that the bat "allowed a batter to hit a ball at speeds in excess of that which would have given a pitcher time to avoid being hit," and thus substantially increased the risk of the pitcher's being hit.

The plaintiff also offered the testimony of an expert who, based on a review of the "evidence," opined that the ball causing

---

8. The product liability claim against U.S.C. and the Pac-10 was subsequently struck by Andrew, and therefore was not part of the case as it moved forward on appeal.

the injury was traveling between 101 and 107.8 miles an hour. The evidence reviewed by the expert, according to the court, included a review of a videotape of the plaintiff's pitching prior to the date of the accident and some deposition transcripts. The expert calculated that the plaintiff had between .32 and .37 seconds to avoid being hit. This reduced reaction time, it was argued, was less than the minimum reaction time of .39 seconds accepted by the NCAA.

The superior court granted the motions of H&B, USC, and the Pac-10 on the theory that the plaintiff could not prove the bat was defective or was the cause of the accident. Among other things, the plaintiff did not establish the speed of the pitch, the speed of the ball leaving the bat, or the position of the pitcher. Therefore, the increased risk associated with the Air Attack 2 was not proven.

The court refused to grant the NCAA its motion for summary judgment because it failed to submit admissible evidence. Notwithstanding this evidentiary problem, it treated the NCAA's motion as a motion for a judgment on the pleadings and concluded that the plaintiff could not "truthfully plead causation."

The plaintiff was called "out." But he challenged the "call" by appealing to the California Court of Appeal for the Second District.

The Court of Appeal Reverses the "Call"

The court of appeal concluded that the evidence offered by the plaintiff was sufficient to create a triable issues of fact as to the application of primary assumption of the risk and causation. The plaintiff was still in the game.

The court of appeal reasoned that the plaintiff had produced sufficient evidence to raise triable issues of fact as to whether the Air Attack 2 bat did significantly increase the inherent risk of harm to Andrew being hit by a line drive, and the related issue of whether the design of the bat was the cause of his injury.

The plaintiff had offered witness and expert declarations to support his increased risk argument. For example, Jack Mackay, the employee-inventor of the bat, testified about the increased risk posed by its design. Jack also revealed that he had complained to H&B about the increased risk of injury associated with using the bat and, thus, they were on notice. Rather than taking action to address the complaint, Jack was told by H&B that he should not publicly discuss "issues of safety." In addition to Jack's testimony, the plaintiff produced other witnesses. Another expert opined that the ball was traveling at a speed faster than the acceptable minimum reaction time accepted by the NCAA and "other organizations."

Although a defendant may owe no duty to protect a voluntary participant from the risks inherent to the game, a defendant does owe a duty not to increase the risk of injury beyond that inherent to the game. Therefore, a key issue to be decided on remand was whether the defendants increased the risk of harm above that inherent in the game of baseball. If the risk of harm was increased, the principles of comparative fault applied under California law.

In deciding whether a risk is inherent to the game, the court of appeal offered two guideposts. First, would the elimination of the risk "chill vigorous participation in the sport"? Second, would the elimination of the risk alter the "fundamental nature" of the game?

There was still the problem of causation because the actual speed of the ball that hit Andrew was never established. The court of appeal responded that the evidence on speed was sufficient to create a triable question of fact. The court referred to the declaration of James G. Kent, a Ph.D in kinesiology:

Based on his training and review of the evidence, he opined that the ball which struck appellant's head was traveling between 101 and 107.8 miles an hour, probably closer to the latter speed than the former. This would have left appellant a reaction time of .32 to .37 seconds to avoid the ball. This was below the minimum reaction time accepted by the NCAA and other organizations of .39 seconds. As a result, he concluded that appellant's head injury resulted from the increased danger posed by this particular bat.

As a result, the court of appeal reversed and remanded the matter to the trial court.

Brett v. Hillerich & Bradsby Co. is an instructively similar case.[9] This time it was a high school pitcher, Jeremy Brett, who was injured by a comeback ball hit by an Air Attack 2 bat. Like Andrew in the *Sanchez* case, Jeremy argued that H&B should be

---

9. Brett v. Hillerich & Bradsby, Case No. CIV-99-981-C, 2001 WL 36162669 (W.D. Okla. Oct. 29, 2001).

held legally accountable for his injuries. H&B predictably argued that Jeremy Brett failed to prove both causation and that the bat was defective. The jury disagreed and awarded him $100,000 in damages for his injuries.

The trial court in *Brett* refused to grant H&B its motion for judgment as a matter of law reasoning that the jury had ample evidence to support the position that the bat was defective because it increased performance beyond that reasonably contemplated by Jeremy. According to the court, there was ample evidence that "the enhanced performance characteristics of the bat caused the injury."

Performance Regulation and Metal Bat Bans

The issue of regulating the performance of metal bats continues to be controversial. In 2000, Jack Mackay filed a petition with the U.S. Consumer Protection Agency requesting it issue a federal rule requiring that all non-wood baseball bats perform like wood bats.[10] He argued that "non-wood bats (primarily made of aluminum and composite materials) have become increasingly dangerous," and therefore present an unreasonable risk of injury.

The commission docketed his request as a petition under the Consumer Product Safety Act and published a notice in the *Federal Register* on June 15, 2000, to solicit comments on the petition from interested persons. On December 28, 2001, the staff sent a briefing package to the commission for its consideration as to whether to grant, deny, or defer the petition. The commission voted to deny the petition on March 6, 2002.

The safety problem may be becoming less acute. Metal bats

---

10. 65 Fed. Reg. 37,526 (June 15, 2000).

now approved for play by the NCAA and the National Federation of State High School Associations must pass a performance standard. Among other standards, bats are required to have a ball-exit-speed-ratio equal to or less than that of a wood bat. This standard significantly reduces the performance attributes of today's metal bats compared to the one used in *Sanchez*.

Nevertheless, some leagues and conferences have banned the use of aluminum bats. In addition, states have considered legislatively banning metal bats. Montana, for example, considered banning them, but ultimately rejected the idea.

At the local level, the "ban the metal bat" movement has gained traction. In 2007, New York City, for example, adopted the following ordinance prohibiting their use by high-school age students in competitive baseball games.

Prohibition of use of non-wood bats:

a. Definitions. When used herein, the following terms shall have the following meanings:

1. "Competitive baseball game" shall mean any organized baseball game at which a certified umpire officiates and which takes place in the city of New York.

2. "High school age children" shall mean persons older than thirteen years of age, but younger than eighteen years of age.

3. "School" shall mean any public or private school which includes any grade nine through twelve and which is located in the city of New York.

4. "Wood bat" shall mean any baseball bat constructed exclusively of wood or any wood laminated or wood composite bat, which is approved by major league baseball, pursuant to such organization's official rules, for major league or minor league baseball

play; provided that such term shall not include any bat made in whole or in part of metal, including, but not limited to, aluminum, magnesium, scandium, titanium or any other alloy compound.

b. Only wood bats shall be used in any competitive baseball game in which high school age children are participants and which involves the participation and/or sponsorship of a school.[11]

The legislative findings accompanying the ordinance state: "The Council hereby finds that the use of non-wood bats poses an unacceptable risk of injury to children, particularly those who play competitive high school baseball."

The constitutionality of the ordinance was challenged in *USA Baseball v. City of New York*.[12] The plaintiffs, who included coaches and parents of New York City high school baseball players, manufacturers of sporting goods, the National High School Baseball Coaches Association, and USA Baseball, which is an organization devoted to promoting amateur baseball, argued that the ordinance violated the due process and equal protection clauses of the federal and state constitutions. Among other arguments, they claimed that there was no empirical evidence to support the city's claim that the ordinance would meet the stated safety objective. Therefore, the ordinance did not have a legally required rational relationship to a legitimate government purpose. They asked the court to enjoin the enforcement of the bat ordinance.

The federal district court rejected the plaintiffs' arguments. It held that the ordinance had a rational relationship to the legitimate purpose of protecting public safety. The court reasoned:

---

11. N.Y.C. ADMIN. CODE § 10-165 (2007).
12. USA Baseball v. City of New York, 509 F. Supp. 2d 285 (S.D.N.Y. 2007).

The plaintiffs seek to discount any possibility of enhanced risk due to batted-ball exit speed in light of the current NCAA and NFHS guidelines that reduced non-wood bats' exit speeds. The plaintiffs then attempt to place the evidentiary burden on the City to produce scientific evidence that the current guidelines are insufficient to protect students. This entire approach is wrong under rational basis review. The City had a rational basis for its distinction based upon the testimony and studies presented to it even if its ultimate choice could be disputed. Moreover, it is unnecessary to focus only on exit speeds, which the plaintiffs assert are now on a relative par between wood bats and metal and composite bats, to see that a rational basis exists for legislatively determining that metal and composite bats could nonetheless result in an increased risk of injury to infielders from hard-struck balls.

The broader point underlying the analysis is straightforward. A court is likely to uphold a legislative determination that non-wood bats are unsafe as long as there is an arguable basis for such a conclusion. A court will defer to the legislative judgment when a rational or debatable basis for the legislation exists.

The controversy over the use of metal bats in baseball will continue. One thing seems clear: Banning them will not ensure that pitchers will avoid being hit by line drives. Wood bats can be every bit as dangerous. Just ask Chris Young.

Umpire's Ruling

Causation under the Rules

As the *Sanchez* case shows, "causation" is important in law. It isn't enough to show that a person acted negligently; one also must show that the negligence caused the injuries for which damages are sought. In criminal law, if two people, acting independently, try to shoot and kill a person, and only one bullet hits the victim, only the shooter whose bullet caused death will be guilty of murder, though the other shooter will be guilty of the lesser crime of attempted murder. In the parlance of the criminal law, murder is a "result" crime (for which causation of the result must be established), but attempted murder is not.

A similar distinction occurs under the Rules of Baseball. Some rules specify penalties regardless of the result of the violation. For example, assume that, with a runner on first, the batter hits what is commonly called a "ground-rule double"—a drive that bounces over the outfield fence. The rules specify that the base runner must stop at third base, even if the runner clearly would have scored had the ball not left the field of play, and that the batter must stop at second, again regardless of what would have happened if the ball had hit the fence and remained in play. In other words, the umpire is not asked to determine whether the ball's leaving the field of play "caused" the batter/runner not to reach third or the runner not to reach home—the rule simply specifies the consequence of the ball's leaving the field of play.

On the other hand, the rules sometimes require umpires to speculate about causation. For example, in the case of interference by a fan with a thrown or batted ball—as when a fan reaches into the field of play—the rules provide that "the ball shall be dead at the moment of interference and the umpire shall impose such penalties as in his opinion will nullify the act of interference."[1] Likewise, when a fielder "obstructs" a base runner, the umpire shall "impose such penalties, if any, as in his judgment will nullify the act of obstruction."[2]

Umpire's Ruling (continued)

This seemingly inconsistent treatment might be justified as follows: Asking umpires to speculate as to what might have happened injects uncertainty and inconsistency into the game, and places the umpires in a difficult situation. When a hard-and-fast rule will generally do justice—and perhaps the ground-rule double example fits—then it is better to avoid this speculation. But other rule violations occur in such varied circumstances that no fixed "penalty" will seem correct enough of the time, and so counterfactual inquiries by the umpire are better in those domains than would be the alternative. (And if obstruction always led to a base runner's being allowed to advance only one base, the smart play would be for the first baseman to tackle a batter on any drive to the gap.)

Also like the criminal law, some of the rules are violated only when a harm results, but others are violated by the attempt to cause the harm. For example, if a pitcher intentionally throws at a batter, the pitcher can be ejected, whether the batter is hit or not.[3] Likewise, the pitcher is to be immediately ejected from the game if found to have, "on his person, or in his possession, any foreign substance," regardless of whether is has been applied to a baseball.[4] And a player, manager, or coach can be ejected from the game for "[c]all[ing] 'Time,' or employ[ing] any other word or phrase or commit[ing] any act while the ball is alive and in play for the obvious purpose of trying to make the pitcher commit a balk," regardless of whether the pitcher commits a balk.[5]

On the other hand, the rules against deflecting a ball with a cap or with a thrown glove impose no penalties unless the fielder succeeds in hitting the ball.[6] The difference in treatment may be partially explained by the practicalities of enforcement. The umpire will usually be able to determine whether a thrown glove deflected a ball. But it will often be difficult to determine whether a pitcher has doctored a ball, so when the pitcher is found in possession of a foreign substance, that fact may often be the best proof for which we can hope. In a noisy stadium, it may often be difficult to determine whether players have engaged in conduct that causes a balk; so when we catch a player trying to do so, we need to punish the conduct severely. And the serious dangers associated with a beanball war justify taking strong action against conduct that could easily escalate, even if the first missile misses.

---

1. Rule 3.16.
2. Rule 7.06(a)-(b).
3. Rule 8.02(d).
4. Rule 8.02(b).
5. Rule 4.06(a)(3).
6. Rule 7.05(b)-(e) Comment.

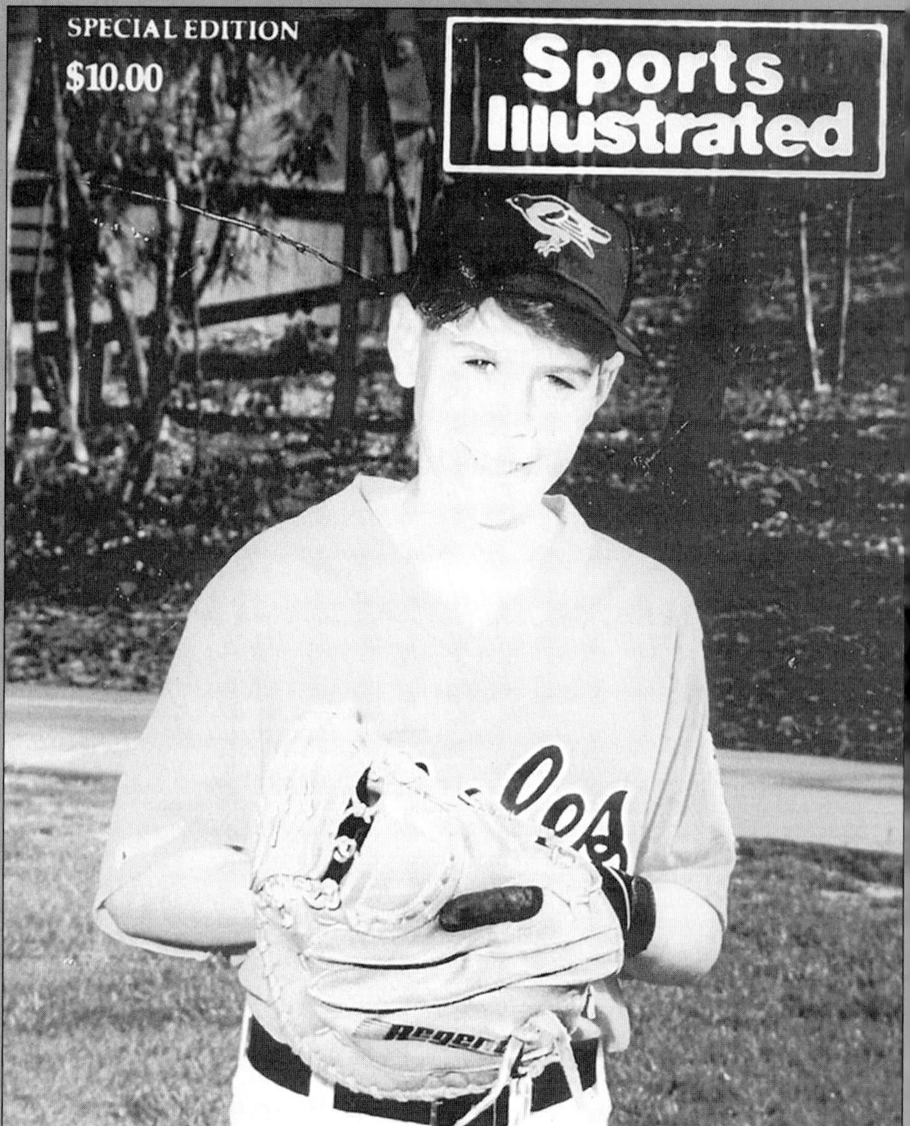

SPECIAL EDITION
$10.00

Sports Illustrated

1992 PLA
THE YE

COVER PHOTO BY
LL AMERICAN COLOR
CTORY 1-800-878-FOTO

The "Beanball," "Brushback," or "Chin Music"

Avila v. Citrus Community College District,
41 Cal. Rptr. 3d 299 (2006)[1]

An umpire necessarily uses judgment in calling balls and strikes. Although fans may disagree with a particular call or series of calls by the umpire, the standard for defining the "strike zone" is clear. It is "the area over home plate the upper limit of which is a horizontal line at the midpoint between the top of the shoulders and the top of the uniform pants, and the lower level is a line at the hollow beneath the kneecap." The area is framed by the stance of the batter when ready to swing at the pitch.[2]

---

1. *Available at* http://www.declarationsandexclusions.typepad.com/weblog/files/s119575_avila_v.%20Citrus.pdf (last visited Sept. 28, 2008).

2. The way the strike zone is defined by major league baseball has changed over the years. Among the changes were the following:

1996—The strike zone is expanded on the lower end, moving from the top of the knees to the bottom of the knees.

1988—The strike zone is that area over home plate the upper limit of which is a horizontal line at the midpoint between the top of the shoulders and the top of the uniform pants, and the lower level is a line at the top of the knees. The strike zone shall be determined from the batter's stance as the batter is prepared to swing at a pitched ball.

1969—The strike zone is that space over home plate which is between the batter's armpits and the top of his knees when he assumes a natural stance. The umpire shall determine the strike zone according to the batter's usual stance when he swings at a pitch.

For a complete historical time line of changes to the strike zone, see http://www.mlb.mlb.com/mlb/official_info/umpires/strike_zone.jsp (last visited July 10, 2008).

A batter may crowd home plate in order to reach the outside portion of the strike zone. A pitcher may respond by throwing an inside "brushback" pitch, sometimes called "chin music." Inside pitches force the batter to back off the plate or risk getting hit by the ball. Batters have responded by wearing protective armor. This give-and-take at the plate is simply part of the game of baseball.

Tragic accidents can happen as the strike-zone minuet between the pitcher and batter progresses. In 1920, for example, the Indians shortstop Ray Chapman was killed after being hit in the head by a wild pitch thrown by New York Yankee Carl Mays at the Polo Grounds in New York.[3] It was the era before batting helmets provided some safety to batters, but the point is still the same. There are certain inherent risks that participants assume when playing the game.

Brushback pitches and wild pitches are obvious risks assumed by the batter. But what about "beanballs"? This type of pitch is thrown by the pitcher, often out of anger or in retaliation, with the intent to hit the batter. Should the law step in and umpire the legality of its use?

When the pitcher intentionally throws at the hitter, the pitcher could, at least in theory, be prosecuted by the state for the

---

3. The following day, Aug. 17, 1920, *The New York Times* reported the following:

Mays is greatly shocked over the accident. He said he threw a high fastball at a time when Chapman was crouched over the plate. He thought the ball hit the handle of Chapman's bat, for he fielded the ball and tossed it to first base. It wasn't until after that, when he saw Umpire Connelly calling to the stands for a physician, that he realized he had hit Chapman in the head. Manager Miller Huggins of the Yankees believes Chapman's left foot may have caught in the ground in some manner which prevented him from stepping out of the ball's way. Manager Huggins explained that batsmen usually had one foot loose and free at just such moments and Chapman had got out of the way of the same kind of pitched balls before.

Available at http://www.nytimes.com/packages/html/sports/year_in_sports/08.17. html (last visited July 7, 2008).

crime of battery.[4] Criminal prosecution, however, is rare. The beanball is not a high priority for prosecutors. Proving the necessary criminal intent would be difficult. Moreover, convincing a jury that the pitcher should be convicted, and perhaps sent to the hoosegow, is also a problem.

The injured batter might sue civilly and attempt to recover damages. In such a situation, the most likely theory is the intentional tort of battery. But as *Avila* illustrates, recovery is not likely.

The beanball is not something new. Pitchers have been throwing at batters for most of the game's history. For example, Don Drysdale, the 1962 Cy Young Award winning pitcher for the Dodgers, was known for using retaliatory measures. When one of his teammates was hit by an opposing pitcher, Drysdale admitted to using a two-to-one retaliation ratio: "If they knocked two of your guys down, I'd get four. You have to protect your hitters."[5] According to Drysdale's contemporary, Mike Shannon,[6] the "Big D" considered an intentional walk a waste of three pitches. "If he wants to put you on base, he can hit you with one pitch." More recent MLB pitchers, such as Roger Clemens, Randy Johnson, and Pedro Martínez, are notoriously known as "headhunters."

Intentionally throwing at the hitter is obviously dangerous to the batter. Moreover, the response to it can rapidly escalate into

---

4. A battery is any willful and unlawful use of force or violence upon the person of another. The government must prove that the defendant intentionally did an act that resulted in harmful or offensive contact with the plaintiff's person, the plaintiff did not consent to the contact, and the contact caused injury, damage, loss or harm to the plaintiff. CAL. PENAL CODE § 242 (2008).

5. *Available at* http://www.baseball-almanac.com/quotes/quodrys.shtml (last visited July 3, 2008).

6. Mike Shannon played for the St. Louis Cardinals and then went on to be a baseball commentator. He is well known for his baseball aphorisms, such as, "you can't sweep a doubleheader if you don't win the first game," and "he's faster than a chicken being chased by Ronald McDonald."

further violence. The opposing team's pitcher may respond in kind through retaliation, the batter may charge the pitcher's mound seeking retribution, or the batter's teammates may swarm the field in a bench-clearing dustup.

The brushback pitches thrown by Giants' pitcher Juan Marichal at Dodgers' Maury Willis and Ron Fairly during the 1965 pennant race precipitated one of the more notorious clashes in baseball history. When Marichal came to bat, Dodgers catcher John Roseboro tossed some "throws back" to Dodgers' pitcher Sandy Koufax that almost took Marichal's nose off. After a brief argument, Marichal resolved the retaliatory action by hitting Roseboro in the head with his bat and spilling blood everywhere. Violence begets violence.

The rules of major league baseball (MLB) prohibit a pitcher

from intentionally throwing at the batter and provide sanctions for failing to following the rule.[7] The rules of the National Collegiate Athletic Association (NCAA) do the same. Rule 5 states:

Pitcher Intentionally Throwing at a Batter—If a pitcher is ejected for intentionally throwing at a batter, the following penalties shall be enforced:

(1) For the first offense by the individual, ejection plus suspension from the team's next four regularly scheduled contests.

(2) For a second offense by the individual in the same season, ejection plus suspension from the team's next eight regularly scheduled contests.

(3) For a third offense by the individual in the same season, ejection plus suspension for the remainder of the season, including postseason competition.

(4) If the coach has been warned during or before the contest, the coach also shall be ejected and suspended for the next regularly scheduled contest (one game).

A.R. 1 The suspended pitcher shall not be allowed to participate in any manner during the suspension.

---

7. The rules of MLB prohibit trying to hit the batter. Rule 8.02(d) states that:

The pitcher shall not—Intentionally Pitch at the Batter.

If, in the umpire's judgment, such a violation occurs, the umpire may elect either to:

1. Expel the pitcher, or the manager and the pitcher, from the game, or

2. May warn the pitcher and the manager of both teams that another such pitch will result in the immediate expulsion of that pitcher (or a replacement) and the manager.

If, in the umpire's judgment, circumstances warrant, both teams may be officially "warned" prior to the game or at any time during the game.

Rule 8.02(d) Comment. To pitch at a batter's head is unsportsmanlike and highly dangerous. It should be—and is—condemned by everybody. Umpires should act without hesitation in enforcement of this rule.

Available at http://www.mlb.mlb.com/mlb/downloads/y2008/official_rules/08_the_pitcher.pdf (last visited July 3, 2008).

A.R. 2 If a pitcher has been ejected while pitching, the substitute shall be allowed an adequate time to warm up, similar to the time allowed when an injured pitcher is replaced.[8]

Although the rules of baseball deal with the beanball, the courts may also be called in to sort things out. In 2006, for example, the California Supreme Court weighed in on the issue in *Avila v. Citrus Community College District.* The court analyzed the reach of legal accountability after a collegiate player was hit in the head and injured by a pitch that was either intentionally thrown to hit the batter or negligently thrown.

The Facts

A 2001 pre-season intercollegiate baseball game was the setting for the case. José Avila, the plaintiff, was playing for the Rio Hondo Community College Roadrunners. Shortly before coming to bat, the pitcher for the Roadrunners hit a batter playing for the opposing team, the Citrus College Owls. Retaliation against the Roadrunners for the offense was on the horizon.

When José came to bat at the top of the next inning, the pitcher for the Owls allegedly hit José in the head in retaliation. The ball was thrown so hard that it cracked his helmet. José went to first base on his own without assistance. When he got there, he complained to his first-base coach that he was in pain and felt dizzy. He was told to stay in the game. After advancing to second base, José was still in pain. Shortly thereafter, he was replaced by a pinch runner and left the game.

José alleged that he suffered "unspecified serious personal injuries" from getting hit. Rather than suffer in silence, José sued

---

8. *Available at* http://www.ncaa.org/library/rules/2006/2006_baseball_rules.pdf (last visited July 3, 2008).

the Citrus Community College District, along with other named defendants,[9] in the Superior Court for Los Angeles County. Among other legal theories, he argued that the district should be found liable for the intentional tort of battery and for negligence.

The district offered two defenses. First, it argued that, as a public entity, it was entitled to immunity from tort claims under the statutory law of California. Second, it argued that it had no duty to supervise the pitcher for the Owls, and therefore could not be held accountable in tort for the pitcher's actions.

The superior court agreed with the district, and dismissed the complaint. José challenged the court's call by going to the court of appeal. The appellate court reversed, saying that the immunity statute did not apply and that the district owed a duty of supervision. Unlike the MLB rule that prohibits a manager from arguing a reversed call after the umpires meet on the field to discuss a play, the district disagreed with the court of appeal. The district asked the California Supreme Court to reverse the court of appeal.

Public Entity Tort Liability

The courts of appeal in California had reached different conclusions on proper application of the immunity statute when applying it to claims against schools and universities. One line of cases said it applied, another said it did not. The court was asked to settle the matter.

The starting point is the language of the statute. The California Government Code section dealing with claims against public entities, such as the district, provides:

---

9. José sued both schools, his manager, the helmet manufacturer, and various other organizations. Only the claims against the district were considered by the Supreme Court.

Neither a public entity nor a public employee is liable to any person who participates in a hazardous recreational activity . . . for any damage or injury to property or persons arising out of that hazardous recreational activity.[10]

The term "hazardous recreational activity" is defined in the section as "a recreational activity conducted on property of a public entity which creates a substantial (as distinguished from a minor, trivial, or insignificant) risk of injury to a participant or a spectator." The term "hazardous recreational activities" covers a laundry list of activities, including "body contact sports," but baseball was not on the list.

The court found the text ambiguous. The term "recreational," which is central to correctly applying the immunity provision, is susceptible to varying interpretations. According to the court, pitching for a professional baseball team would not be considered "recreational," but pitching for an adult amateur softball team would be recreational.

A collegiate game seemed to fit somewhere in between. Thus, it was not clear from the text whether school-sponsored extracurricular athletics fit within the meaning of "recreational activity." Should it matter whether José was on a scholarship or required to participate as part of a physical education requirement?

The court consulted the legislative purpose of the immunity provision. The legislative history indicated that the statute was designed to limit a public entity's liability for failing either to maintain public property or to warn of dangerous conditions on public property. Therefore, the court reasoned, that immunity for public entities was intended by the legislature to exist only for

---

10. CAL. GOV'T CODE § 831.7(a) (2008).

those injuries sustained by members of the public during "voluntary unsupervised play on public land."

The statute was not intended to limit the liability of a public entity from other duties, such as the duty to supervise activities. Therefore, the court found that school sports in general, and organized intercollegiate games in particular, were not "recreational" within the meaning of the immunity statute. As a result, the district was not entitled to the liability shield created by the immunity statute.

The court expressly refused to decide whether unsupervised intramural or club matches fell within the protection of the statute. It did, however, state that to the extent other case law suggests that the immunity statute "*always* immunizes universities against liability for injuries sustained by their adult student-athletes, we disapprove it."

Primary Assumption of the Risk

Finding that the district was not immune from liability under the statute did not the end the analysis. An important question remained: Did the district breach its duty not to enhance the inherent risks of the game?

In the sports context, primary assumption of the risk precludes liability for injuries arising from those risks inherent to the sport. The court previously had recognized that an athlete does not assume the risk of a co-participant's intentional or reckless conduct outside the range of ordinary conduct involved in the sport.

Nevertheless, the court concluded that, when a person is batting, "being intentionally thrown at is a fundamental part and inherent risk of the sport of baseball." Being hit by a pitch therefore is an inherent risk of the game. The player who steps to the plate consents to the possibility that a pitcher may throw near or at him.

The court looked to professional baseball for support:

> Pitchers intentionally throw at batters to disrupt a batter's timing or back him away from home plate, to retaliate after a teammate has been hit, or to punish a batter for having hit a home run. Some of the most respected baseball managers and pitchers have openly discussed the fundamental place throwing at batters has in their sport. In George Will's study of the game, *Men at Work*, one-time Oakland Athletics and current St. Louis Cardinals manager Tony La Russa details the strategic importance of ordering selective intentional throwing at opposing batters, principally to retaliate for one's own players being hit.

The court saw no reason to distinguish between collegiate and professional baseball in applying primary assumption of the risk principles.

It is one thing for the umpire to eject a pitcher or the league to suspend the pitcher. It is another matter for the law to step in. Applying the law of torts, according to the court, would have the potential of changing the nature of the game. Even assuming the pitcher intentionally threw at the batter, the conduct does not fall outside the range of ordinary activities involved in the game. Consequently, the district owed José no duty to prevent a pitcher from hitting batters, even intentionally.

José's complaint did not expressly allege that the coach had ordered or allowed the beanball. The inherent-risk analysis suggests that the outcome might not have been different had he done so. The batter consents to the possibility that the opposing pitcher may throw at or near him or her.

In California, any remedy for intentionally throwing a ball at a batter during an intercollegiate baseball game is now left to the umpires to sort out, not the courts. The beanball appears to be an inherent risk of the game and, therefore, outside the law of negligence as well as intentional torts.

Pitchers have been throwing at batters for most of baseball's history, and the California Supreme Court wasn't about to change the rules of the game. In short, "it is not the function of tort law to police such conduct."

Umpire's Ruling

Protecting the Batter

In addition to the rule forbidding intentionally throwing at batters, the rules also were amended to require the use of batting helmets beginning in 1971—over 50 years after the death of Ray Chapman. Even then, players who had already appeared in the major leagues were permitted to play without wearing helmets. The last player to bat without a helmet in the major leagues was Bob Montgomery in 1979.[1] In the early 1980s, the rules were amended again to require players to wear a helmet with an ear flap, which provides additional protection. Again, players already in the big leagues were permitted to opt out of the ear-flap requirement.

While the gravity of a player's being hit in the head has led MLB progressively to increase protection, the story of the elbow pad shows a willingness to let fear of the ball play a role in baseball. Like MLB home run leader Barry Bonds, many players in the late 1990s and early 2000s were wearing substantial body armor on their lead arms (the right arm for a left-handed hitter like Bonds). In many ways, these pads may have been more helpful to the hitter than the helmet. MLB hitters will generally not think that their head is in danger from a pitch that ends up in the strike zone. But the lead arm is much closer to the hitting area, and protecting the arm skews the balance of power toward the hitter.

MLB ultimately adopted a rule generally limiting elbow pads to 10 inches in length and requiring that they be covered in nylon rather than a harder material. A player may wear a longer pad, or one designed to protect the upper or lower arm, only with a doctor's note indicating the pad is needed to protect an existing injury. Unlike most Rules, this one is not enforced by the umpires during a game. Rather, claimed violations of the rule are reported to the league office for investigation and possible discipline.[2]

---

1. http://www.en.wikipedia.org/wiki/Batting_helmet.
2. http://www.mlb.mlb.com/mlb/official_info/umpires/rules_interest.jsp; http://www.espn.go.com/mlb/news/2002/0318/1353635.html.

Stockpiling Trademarks and the "Hall of Shame"

Central Manufacturing, Inc. v. George Brett and Brett Bros., 492 F.3d 876 (7th Cir. 2007)

A Nostalgic Look Back

George Brett is a recognized baseball legend. In 1999, he was inducted into the National Baseball Hall of Fame in Cooperstown, New York. During his long-running career with the Kansas City Royals, he had 3,154 hits, 317 home runs, and a career batting average of .305.

George is also well known for the "pine tar incident," which became known in the baseball world as "Tar Wars." During the summer of 1983, he was batting against Rich "Goose" Gossage, another hall-of-famer. Gossage was pitching for the New York Yankees. It was the top of the ninth inning, with two outs, and one runner on base. The Royals were trailing the Yankees 4-3. When all that was left was hopes and prayers for the Royals, George smacked a massive home run. The Royals won 5-4. Or did they?

Billy Martin, the firebrand coach of the Yankees, demanded that Tim McClelland, the home plate umpire, check George's bat for pine tar, which is a sticky substance used to improve a player's grip on the bat.

At the time, the Official Baseball Rule 1.10(b) provided that "the bat handle, for not more than 18 inches from the end, may be covered or treated with any material (including pine tar) to improve the grip. Any such material, including pine tar, which extends past the 18 inch limitation, in the umpire's judgment, shall cause the bat to be removed from the game. No such material shall improve the reaction or distance factor of the bat."

After examining the bat, the umpire ruled that the pine tar exceeded the 18-inch limit. The pine tar covered about 24 inches on the handle. McClelland declared the bat illegal, and George's home run was nullified. The Yankees won 4-3, or did they?

George burst from the dugout and attempted to perform some serious chiropractic moves on McClelland. George also served up a fiery string of invocations not heard during regular church services. He was ejected from the game. George's teammate, Gaylord Perry, grabbed the bat from the umpire and headed for the clubhouse with members of the umpiring staff and stadium security in hot pursuit so that the contraband could be impounded and delivered to the league office the following morning.

Lee MacPhail, the American League president, agreed to reconsider McClelland's ruling. Several days after researching the rules and weighing them, MacPhail concluded that the McClelland was wrong. Although he found McClelland's ruling "technically defensible," it did not comport with either the intent or spirit underlying the rules. The bat was not altered by George to improve "the distance factor." The outcome, he reasoned, ought to be determined on the field of play and not by the technicalities of the rules. Much like decisions by the U.S. Supreme Court, no further appeal was possible.

To use a phrase familiar to appellate lawyers, MacPhail "reversed and remanded for further proceedings." Several weeks later, on August 18, play resumed with the Royals in the lead 5-4. But George and others had been ejected for their "overly aggressive reaction" to the call by McClelland. After the Royals's closer Dan Quisenberry retired the Yankees in the bottom of the ninth after 12 minutes of resumed play, the Royals marched from the field with a 5-4 victory.

George Brett and Another Baseball Bat

Joe Sample was a man with an idea. He saw a market niche for bats that had the feel of a wood bat and the durability of a metal bat. In 1997, Joe created Tridiamond Sports, Inc. and set to work developing a specialized process to laminate and fiberglass a bat that combined feel and durability. The product line he established included three models: the Mirador, the Bomber, and the Stealth. It was a technological leap forward.

In 2001, George Brett and Tridiamond Sports formed Brett Brothers Sports International, Inc. (Brett Brothers). The company sells different models of wood bats used by amateur and professional baseball players. The Brett Bros. Web site describes the Stealth model:

> The stealth bats are constructed of laminates from hand selected and graded hardwoods. The patented "Boa" reinforcement on the handle significantly enhances durability. The choice of wood for the barrel has proven to greatly reduce the chipping and flaking characteristic in one-piece ash bats.
>
> This model has NCAA approval for all levels of play and is also BESR Certified.

The Stealth bat is available in 31", 32", 33", and 34" lengths with a weight drop of - 3 oz.[1]

The first sale of Stealth bats was in 1999, and since then Brett Bros. has sold more than 25,000 Stealth bats.

Things Get Sticky

In 1984, Leo Stoller registered the "Stealth" trademark with the U.S. Patent and Trademark Office (PTO) for baseballs and other products. The mark was awarded by the PTO in 1985.

In 2001, Stoller also filed a trademark application with the PTO for use of "Stealth" on "baseball bats, softball bats and t-ball bats." In 2004, five years after the first sale of Stealth bats by Brett Bros., the PTO granted Leo the trademark for Stealth bats.

Things got sticky when Stoller sent Brett Bros. a cease-and-desist letter claiming ownership of the "Stealth" mark for use on bats and demanding a $100,000 licensing fee. Brett Bros. refused both to stop using the Stealth name or to pay the fee. As a result, Leo Stoller, who controlled both Central Manufacturing, Inc. and Stealth Industries, Inc., sued George Brett and Brett Bros. in the U.S. District Court for the Northern District of Illinois for infringement under the Lanham Act and state law. The court granted summary judgment to the Brett Bros., and Stoller appealed to the Seventh Circuit.

Although registration of a trademark is prima facie evidence of ownership, it is not conclusive. To be protected, the registrant must actually use the mark in commerce. This requirement prevents a registrant from simply getting a trademark for the purpose of making another pay for the privilege of using it. The pur-

---

1. *Available at* http://www.shopsite.brettbats.com/shopbats.html (last visited Feb. 18, 2008).

"YOU'LL HAVE TO CHANGE YOUR STANCE. A PLAYER ON THE WHITE SOX CLAIMS IT'S HIS INTELLECTUAL PROPERTY."

pose of trademark law is to promote and protect commerce. It is not to allow registrants to profit by stockpiling trademarks.

Stoller argued that his rights predated Brett Bros. The 1985 "Stealth" registration, he claimed, predated Brett Bros.'s use by five years. There was, however, a problem with the argument. Stoller's 1985 PTO registration was for "baseballs and other sporting goods" and not for bats. He attempted to finesse this difficulty by arguing that the registration also included bats on the theory bats were "closely related products."

Brett Bros. were not impressed. Rather than arguing about bats and balls, they said that the trademark was not protected in the first place because the mark was never used in commerce. This was the chiropractic move that made the difference. The Seventh Circuit agreed with the district court's finding:

Plaintiffs have failed completely to support their claim that they actually used the "Stealth" mark in connection

187

The Little White Book of Baseball Law

with an established, presently existing, and ongoing business prior to Brett Bros. use of the word "Stealth" in 1999.

It was unfathomable that the plaintiffs could not produce a single purchase order or invoice as proof that they were using the mark for more than a decade.

Strikes Two and Three

The Seventh Circuit upheld the district court's cancellation of Stoller's 2005 registration of the Stealth mark for baseball bats. It also awarded Brett Bros. attorneys' fees and defense costs. It found that Stoller's case lacked merit, had elements of an abuse of process, and unreasonably increased the costs of defending the lawsuit by not producing evidence after repeatedly being asked to do so. The documents eventually produced by Stoller "effectively made a mockery of the entire proceeding."

At the time of the litigation, Leo Stoller had registered upwards of 50 trademarks with the PTO, many containing everyday words used in commercial transactions. His apparent business strategy was to use cease-and-desist demand letters in the hope that his targets would pay up, but his general scheme is no longer operational.[2]

If there were a hall of shame for trademark abusers, Stoller would be in it. The Seventh Circuit clearly would have voted him in on the first ballot. Other recipients of his demand letters would have undoubtedly supported his election to the hall of shame.

---

2. In 2007, a federal bankruptcy court approved the sale of Stoller's trademark assets, including the claim to stealth, to the Society for the Prevention of Trademark Abuse, LLC. *Available at* http://home.comcast.net/~jlw28129/SPTA_letter_to_J_Welch.pdf (last visited Oct. 31, 2008).

666

Umpire's Ruling

Doctored Bats

The MLB umpire in the Tar Wars case, Tim McClelland, was also involved in another noteworthy MLB game involving the legality of a bat. As noted in Inning 13, in the major leagues the bat must be made of "one piece of solid wood."[1] Sometimes it isn't.

On June 3, 2003, Sammy Sosa, the Chicago Cubs slugger who had, at that point, hit 505 career home runs, broke his bat on a ground out to second base that appeared to score a runner from third. However, when crew chief McClelland examined the debris, he determined that the bat had been "corked"—a process that can increase the distance a ball travels when hit with a wood bat. Sosa was ejected from the game, declared out, and the base runner was required to return to third base.

Rule 6.06(d) dictated the outcome. It provides that a batter will be declared out if the batter "uses or attempts to use a bat that, in the umpire's judgment, has been altered or tampered with in such a way to improve the distance factor or cause an unusual reaction on the baseball. This includes, bats that are filled, flat-surfaced, nailed, hollowed, grooved or covered with a substance such as paraffin, wax, etc."

Sosa claimed that he did not realize the bat he brought to the plate was corked. He said he used the bat during batting practice to "put on a show for the fans." But Sosa's "defense" didn't prevail. Some of the Rules of Baseball impose penalties only when a player has a culpable mental state, as those that apply when a runner "intentionally" interferes with a batted ball. But many rules apply regardless of the player's mental state. In law, these are called "strict liability" offenses. A pitch is a ball even if the pitcher was trying to throw a strike; likewise, a bat is illegal even if the batter doesn't know it.[2]

The difference between the Sosa case and the Tar Wars case has to do with the likely effect of the violation. The purpose of corking a bat is to hit the ball harder and farther. But pine tar

189

Umpire's Ruling (continued)

beyond 18 inches of the knob is forbidden not because of fear that hitting with pine tar will improve bat performance. Rather, pine tar in the hitting area could be transferred to the ball, leading to erratic throws by fielders when the ball is put in play and increased cost as balls are hit, tainted, and removed from play. Accordingly, after the pine-tar incident, the rules were amended to provide that, when the pine-tar rule is violated and the umpire discovers that fact after the bat has been used to put the ball in play, "it shall not be grounds for declaring the batter out, or ejected from the game."[3]

---

1. Rule 1.10(a).
2. Unsplendid splinter: Cubs rally past Rays after Sosa's ignominious ejection, http://www.sportsillustrated.cnn.com/baseball/news/2003/06/03/sosa_ejected_ap/.
3. Rule 1.10(c).

Umps Reverse Their Employment Call

Major League Umpires Association v.
American League of Professional Baseball Clubs,
357 F.3d 272 (3d Cir. 2004), *cert. denied* (2005)[1]

Major league baseball (MLB) and labor problems, usually over money, go together like too many hot dogs and beers at a ball game. Sometimes they cause indigestion. Since 1972, MLB players have gone on strike or the owners have engaged in a lockout on eight different occasions.[2]

The most traumatic episode was a season-ending strike involving salary caps and revenue sharing. In August 1994, the players went on a labor strike that lasted until March 1995. It led to the World Series being canceled for the first time since 1904. The field of dreams was metaphorically plowed under. The lyrics to Jim Nuzzo's song "The Game Is Over" fit:

> *The game is over before it's begun*
> *The crowds, they're not coming*

---

1. *Available at* http://www.ca3.uscourts.gov/opinarch/021103p.pdf (last visited Sept. 28, 2008).

2. A general description of the labor issues during this period is *available at* http://www.sportsillustrated.cnn.com/baseball/news/2002/05/25/work_stopppages/ (last visited Aug. 8, 2008).

There will be no more fun
Greed and compensation
Are now number one . . . .

Former Commissioner Peter Ueberroth observed: "Baseball games are won and lost because of errors—and this will go down as the biggest 'E' of all. 1994—the season that struck itself out." Fortunately, the federal courts saved the following season.[3]

Labor disputes between the owners and the "boys of summer" have received most of the attention over the years. Yet, labor controversy also has spilled over to the owners and umpires. The "boys in blue" are paid to make difficult judgment calls that are expressly communicated by demonstrative hand gestures and shouting sounds like "HROOUUT!"[4] During a typical nine-inning game, for example, a home plate umpire decides whether 300 or so pitches are "balls" or "strikes." Many of them are close calls made under intense scrutiny.

Unlike players who often are cheered for their performance, umpires rarely receive such cheers. More often than not, the chorus they get from fans is one of "boos," or refrains like "you couldn't call a cab," or other words of endearment, some of which have been put to song.[5]

---

3. Silverman v. Major League Baseball Player Relations Comm., Inc., 67 F.3d 1054 (2d Cir. 1995) (finding that MLB could not unilaterally dispose of salary arbitration without violating a crucial portion of its Collective Bargaining Agreement with the Baseball Players Association).

4. In 2007, MLB reported that a Major League umpire's starting salary was around $120,000, with senior umpires earning up to $350,000. Umps also receive a $340 per-diem travel allowance. *Available at* http://www.mlb.mlb.com/news/article.jsp?ymd=20070827&content_id=2173765&vkey=news_mlb&fext=.jsp&c_id=mlb (last visited Aug. 9, 2008).

5. *The umpire, the umpire, the guy who calls every play.*
We ain't got no use for the umpire unless he calls 'em our way.
Hey Tommy – He calls one a strike that just misses my hat,
And that's how I know that he's blind as a bat.
Ralph – I pitch 'em right over he gives 'em a walk.
I scratch my right ear and he calls it a balk.

The role of an umpire is similar to that of a courtroom judge. In John Roberts's prepared statement to the Senate Judiciary Committee on his nomination to become the Chief Justice of the U.S. Supreme Court, Roberts compared the role of judges to that of umpires:

> Judges are like umpires. Umpires don't make the rules; they apply them. The role of an umpire and a judge is critical. They make sure everybody plays by the rules. But it is a limited role. Nobody ever went to a ball game to see the umpire.[6]

The exercise of judgment by a MLB umpire, such as whether the pitch is a ball or strike or a batted ball is fair or foul, is final. Right or wrong, the umpire's decision stands.[7] A player, manager, or coach who challenges the call risks being ejected from the game. Like most rules, the rules of MLB contain an exception. If reasonable doubt exists as to whether the call conflicts with the rules, the manager may ask the umpire to correct the call.[8]

Phil – I slide into second I'm safe without doubt,
But up goes his thumb and the bum says "You're out."
Roy – I tell him his eyes are not all they should be,
And next thing you know it's the showers for me.
The umpire, the umpire, the guy who calls every play.
We ain't got no use for the umpire unless he calls 'em our way.

Lyrics from the 1952 song "The Umpire," by Mitch Miller.

6. John Roberts's prepared opening statement, Senate Judiciary Committee Hearing, Sept. 12, 2005. *Available at* http://www.traditionalvalues.org/modules.php?sid=2421 (last visited Aug. 3, 2008).

7. This does not mean that decisions are beyond performance review. In 2001, the company QuesTec signed a contract with MLB, which has been renewed annually through 2008, to use its pitch-tracking system to review the performance of home plate umpires. It is not used, however, in all MLB stadiums.

In August 2008, a limited form of instant replay came to baseball. At least for now, video replay will be used by umpires only on so-called "boundary calls," such as determining whether fly balls went over the fence, whether potential home runs were fair or foul, and whether there was fan interference on potential home runs.

8. MLB Rule 9.02.

Umpires take the heat when they make a mistake. In *Major League Umpires Association*, the umpires made a strategic error, which they tried to "correct" through litigation. The principal catalyst to the dispute was umpire accountability. Durwood Merrill, a longtime American League umpire, captured the accountability issue in his book *You're Out and You're Ugly Too!*: "When an umpire establishes his strike zone, everybody in the league had better get ready to deal with it. You have to understand that no two strike zones are the same."

The Setup

The Major League Umpires Association (Association) represents the umpires employed by the American League (AL) and National League (NL). The commissioner of baseball oversees the operation of the leagues and baseball generally.

In 1999, Commissioner "Bud" Selig attempted to implement new policies. The proposed policies included, among others, a system for evaluating the consistency of individual umpires' interpretation of the strike zone and enlisting club general managers to "chart" strike zone pitches.[9]

The Association balked at the policies. It generally saw the proposed policies as a power grab that would strip the league presidents of supervisory power over umpires and centralize power in the commissioner's office. The objections translated into a legal complaint. The Association maintained that the proposed policies violated the existing Collective Bargaining Agreement (CBA) between the Association and the leagues.

What should the Association do? The use of a labor strike or

---

9. QuesTec installed the "Umpire Information System" in 10 MLB parks in 2002. The four-camera system records the position of each pitch and whether it was called a ball or a strike. *Available at* http://www.hardballtimes.com/main/article/the-outside-corner (last visited Sept. 4, 2008).

other form of work stoppage would violate the CBA. Article XIX contained a labor "no-strike" clause whereby the Association agreed that "there shall be no strike or other concerted work stoppage." The CBA also required the Association to use its best efforts to insure that the umpires would faithfully carry out their obligations as employees.

The Resignation Strategy

The Association wanted to force the leagues to negotiate with it over the proposed policies. Because a strike or work stoppage would violate the CBA, it elected to pursue a mass resignation strategy. Although the strategy turned out to be foolish, it seemed sensible at the time because it offered the umpires some financial leverage. Voluntary resignation would obligate the leagues to pay the resigning umpires some $15 million in severance compensation.

At the time, the Association had 68 umpire members. On July 15, 1999, 57 umpires submitted letters of resignation to their respective AL and NL presidents. The relevant part of the form resignation letter said:

> Effective September 2, 1999, I hereby resign from my employment from the [American or National] League pursuant to Article VIII.D of the Basic Agreement between the American League of Professional Baseball Clubs, the National League of Professional Baseball Clubs and the Major League Umpires Association dated January 1, 1995. [Where applicable:] I hereby demand my voluntary termination pay.

On July 22, Commissioner Selig and the league presidents met to discuss the resignations. The leagues decided not to nego-

tiate with the Association, and by the end of the day had hired 20 replacement umpires.

The mass resignation strategy was not working. As a result, some umpires attempted to correct their call by rescinding their letters of resignation. By July 27, the rest of umpires seeing the folly of their ways attempted to recall their resignations en masse. Some who had resigned received a "thank you for your service" and good-luck-in-your-future-endeavors letter. Others were allowed to rescind their letters.

Nearly one-third of the Association's membership were left unemployed—a total of 22 (nine from the American League and 13 from the National League). These umpires were not permitted to rescind their letters of resignation by the leagues.

On August 27, the Association responded by filing a demand for arbitration of its labor grievances. From its perspective, the hiring of replacements by the leagues was nothing short of an effort to break the union, and thus constituted an unfair labor practice that violated the CBA.

Time was running out as the effective-resignation date, September 2, approached. On August 30, two days before the resignations became effective, the Association asked the Federal District Court for the Eastern District of Pennsylvania to enjoin the leagues from accepting those resignations that had not been rescinded.

Following a district court hearing, the Association and the Leagues entered into a Memorandum of Understanding (MOU). It provided that the parties would submit the dispute to arbitration. But the MOU also contained a provision that would subsequently prove troublesome to promptly resolving the disagreement. It provided that either party could argue "whatever procedural and substantive arbitrability arguments" they had.

Arbitrating the Dispute

The Association argued it was entitled to arbitration pursuant to "claimed violations" of the CBA. Article XV states that if an agreement is not reached on a "claimed violation," the dispute "shall be referred to an arbitrator" mutually agreed upon by the parties.

The leagues, on the other hand, argued that the general arbitration provision of Article XV had not been triggered. It maintained that Article VIII of the CBA controlled. Under clause one of this article, the league presidents had the authority to issue a "final and binding" decision on a "discharge" after a hearing.[10]

---

10. Article VIII provides in relevant part in Section A, Tenure:

[1] "In the event an umpire with five or more years of service is discharged by a League President, the umpire and the representative of the Association shall be entitled to an explanation of the reasons for his discharge and the umpire shall be entitled at his request to hearing before the League President at which time the discharge shall be subject to full review and re-examination by the League president. The decision of the League President after such hearing shall be final and binding."

The same article also vested discretion in the league presidents on matters of selection and retention.[11] Therefore, it claimed that the Association's grievance of not being allowed withdraw the letters of resignation was not subject to arbitration.

The arbitrator rejected the league's argument. He found that the Article VIII authority was constrained by the language of the article itself. He saw the issue as one of whether the accepted resignations by the leagues constituted an abuse of discretion, or were discriminatory or recriminatory. These were issues subject to arbitration under the CBA.

In May 2001, the arbitrator issued his opinion stating that he had jurisdiction under the CBA to arbitrate the claimed violations. With this determination in place, he then found that the leagues were entitled to hire replacement umpires in reliance on the letters of resignation. But he also found that nine (two AL and seven NL) umpires were entitled to reinstatement as well as full back pay and benefits. The basis for this reinstatement is not clear from the court records. Nevertheless, the result is clear. Thirteen umpires were not entitled to reinstatement.

Back to the Federal Courts

Both sides were unhappy with the result, but obviously for different reasons. The leagues and Association asked the federal district court to set aside those portions of the arbitrator's award unfavorable to them. The leagues continued to object to arbitrator's jurisdiction.

The district court rejected the jurisdictional objection. It

---

11. Article VIII also provides:

[2] "All umpires shall be selected or retained in the discretion of the League Presidents on the basis of merit and the skill of the umpire to perform to Major League standards. With respect to all such members of the regular staff, there shall be no discrimination or recrimination on the part of any party to this Agreement."

held that "because the parties contracted to arbitrate disputes concerning any 'claimed violation' of the Agreement, and because the current dispute concerning the selection or retention of umpires is such a 'claimed violation,' the arbitrator properly exercised jurisdiction."

The leagues pressed the jurisdictional objection by appealing their "check-swing" to the Third Circuit Court of Appeals. The Third Circuit also rejected its claim. It found that the arbitrator had not exceeded his authority because his award "drew its essence from the CBA." In short, the finding of arbitrability was premised on the alleged violations of the CBA under the general dispute resolution of Article XV.

The Third Circuit exercised considerable analytical gymnastics to support its conclusion affirming the jurisdiction of the arbitrator. Because no umpire was terminated or discharged by the leagues, one has to justify the result by finding the arbitrator had the authority to resolve a "claimed violation" of the CBA. Otherwise, the decision appears clearly erroneous.

The Lesson Learned

The judicial review of an arbitrator's decision pursuant to a CBA is limited. A strong presumption exists in favor of enforcing the arbitrator's interpretation of the agreement, and a court's deferential role in reviewing arbitration awards usually will not allow for its review of the factual or legal merits of an award. In short, a court will vacate a labor arbitration award only in limited circumstances. The one clear basis is where arbitrators exceed their authority. This authority is defined by the CBA as well as by the scope of the issues submitted by the parties to an arbitrator. As shown by *Major League Umpires Association*, an arbitrator's decision is subject to the legal standard of minimal rationality.

Umpire's Ruling

"Wait—I changed my mind"

Just as some of the resigning umpires were bound by their initial decisions, at given points, certain decisions by other participants in the game become irrevocable under the rules.

For example, the home team determines whether to cancel or postpone a game because of weather, but only until it hands its batting order to the umpire-in-chief at the conference immediately preceding the beginning of the game. At that point, the power to make decisions about cancelling or delaying the game belongs to the umpire.[1]

After inspecting the duplicate copies of the batting order provided by the manager to ensure they are identical and that they contain no obvious errors (such as listing too few batters), the umpire shall then "tender a copy of each batting order to the opposing manager." That act sets the starting line-up, and subsequent changes are governed by the substitution rules.[2] Accordingly, the pitcher listed as the starter, unless injured, must pitch to one batter before the manager can make a change.

While youth baseball leagues often have different rules, the official rules state that a player, once removed from the game, cannot re-enter.[3] However, a player may change defensive positions during a game. While it is uncommon at the MLB level, on rare occasions a manager has moved the pitcher to another defensive position so that a reliever can be brought in to face a particular batter, subsequently returning the original pitcher to the mound.

The manager is only allowed to visit the same pitcher once during an inning; on a second visit, the pitcher must be removed. When the manager "leaves the 18-foot circle surrounding the pitcher's rubber," the visit ends. If a forgetful manager goes back to impart forgotten wisdom, that counts as a second visit and requires that the pitcher be removed.[4]

---

1. Rule 4.01(d).
2. Rule 4.01(c).
3. Rule 3.03.
4. Rule 8.06.

The "World Series" of Payroll Tax Litigation

United States v. Cleveland Indians Baseball Company, 532 U.S. 200 (2001)[1]

n 2001, the Cleveland Indians[2] finished first in the Central Division of the American League. In the American League playoffs, they lost to the New York Yankees, who went on to play the Diamondbacks in the 2001 World Series.[3] Off the field, the Indians were singing the tune "Takin' Care of Business" in

---

1. *Available at* http://www.supreme.justia.com/us/532/200/case.html (last visited Sept. 28, 2008).

2. Professional baseball was first played in Cleveland in 1869. In 1901, the Cleveland Spiders ball club became a charter member of the American League of Professional Baseball Clubs. Before the team acquired the name Cleveland Indians in 1915, Cy Young played for Cleveland.

3. The 2001 World Series was especially memorable. The New York Yankees and the Arizona Diamondbacks were locked in an epic battle. The struggle came down to the ninth inning of game seven. Yankee closer Mariano Rivera and the Arizona Diamondbacks' Randy Johnson, two of the best in the game, were locked in a tight pitchers' duel. The Diamondbacks were down 2-1. But the Diamondbacks found some game-ending magic when Luis Gonzalez blooped a single into centerfield over Derek Jeter with the bases loaded. The Diamondbacks won, 3-2. The victory was historic in that the Diamondbacks won a World Series faster than any other expansion club in baseball history.

their fight with the Internal Revenue Service (IRS) over a claim for a tax refund.[4]

In addition to winning the Central Division, the Indians had stacked up a series of wins in the lower federal courts. But the U.S. Supreme Court rejected their tune that it had overpaid Social Security and unemployment taxes. The outcome, although unfavorable to the Indians, did clarify the law on the taxation of labor settlements.

The Early Innings

In 1968, Major League Baseball (MLB) team owners and the Major League Baseball Players Association (MLBPA) negotiated the first-ever Collective Bargaining Agreement (CBA) whereby the MLBPA became the bargaining agent for major league players. In 1990, the MLBPA claimed that the owners breached the CBA with respect to the free-agency rights of the baseball players in 1986, 1987, and 1988. According to the MLBPA, the owners were colluding to keep free agent players' salaries low.

As provided in the CBA, the matter was referred to arbitration. An arbitration panel found that the owners breached Article XVIII(H) of the CBA, which prohibited the owners from taking concerted action to interfere with the free agency rights of their players. The arbitration panel found that the owners violated the CBA at the end of the 1985 and 1986 playing seasons, and that the owners' actions artificially depressed the salaries for would-be free agents in the subsequent seasons. Therefore, the owners were required to pay back wages.

---

4. The song "Takin' Care of Business" is popular with some baseball teams. The New York Mets played it after their victories during the 2006, 2007, and 2008 seasons. The Atlanta Braves, a division rival, played it during their run of 14 consecutive division titles. In the 1990 movie "Taking Care of Business," Jim Belushi plays an irrepressible and always upbeat convict who escapes from prison to attend the World Series.

In late 1990, the parties reached a settlement. Pursuant to the agreement, the owners contributed $280 million to a custodial account for their misdeeds. The payments to the affected players were to be made according to the MLBPA framework.

The Mid-Innings

The Indians were one of 26 MLB clubs found guilty of collusion in not signing free agents. Twenty-three Indians players were eligible to split about $2.7 million of the Cleveland pot. Eight players were employed by the team in 1986 and 15 in 1987.

The Indians paid Federal Insurance Contributions Act (FICA)[5] and Federal Unemployment Tax Act (FUTA)[6] taxes on the payments to the affected players. It treated the payments as "wages" for services rendered in 1994. Although the taxes were paid in April 1994 and January 1995, the IRS agreed to the fact that no services actually were performed by the affected players for the Indians in either 1986 or 1987.

The Indians filed suit against the U.S. Internal Revenue Service (IRS) in the Federal District Court for the Northern District of Ohio seeking a tax refund. First, it argued that some of the back-payments were interest, and not wages subject to either FICA or FUTA tax. The IRS conceded this point, and as a result the Indians received a partial refund of slightly more than $13,000.

The crux of the continuing controversy turned on which tax rate applied. The Indians argued that about $2 million of the back payments should be taxed based on the year they *should* have

---

5. FICA is a tax to fund the federal Social Security program that is imposed upon both employees and employers. It is equal to a percentage of the wages paid by the employer to the employee.

6. FUTA is an excise tax imposed upon employers to fund the federal unemployment program. It is calculated as a percentage of the wages the employer has paid to the employee and varies based on the calendar year for which the wages were paid.

been paid, not the year they were *actually* paid. The tax year made a difference because the tax law had changed. If the back payments were allocated to 1986 and 1987 tax years, the Indians would get a tax refund because both the tax rate and the amount of wages subject to tax (the wage base) had gone up.[7]

The IRS argued the law was clear.[8] It maintained that both the wage base and the tax rate sections of the Internal Revenue Code refer to total wages paid by the employer "during the calendar year." Based on this language, the IRS maintained that wages should be taxed "according to the calendar year in which they are in fact paid, regardless of when they should have been paid."

The IRS also noted that the current language adopted by Congress replaced the earlier language used in the Social Security Act, which referred to wages received with respect to "employment during the calendar year" with the language "wages paid during the calendar year." Congress intended a clarifying change.

The district court rejected the IRS's argument. The text of the tax code was not crystal clear. Relying on its reading of the law, the district court found that the year the wages were earned controlled (1986 and 1987), and not when the payments were made (1994). Therefore, it ordered the IRS to refund approximately

---

7. Social Security taxes were 5.7 percent in 1986 and 1987 but had gone up to 6.2 percent by 1994. Unemployment taxes, which are paid only by the employer, had gone from 6 percent in 1986 and 1987 to 6.2 percent in 1994.

8. The Internal Revenue Code imposes employment taxes "on every employer . . . equal to [a percentage of] wages . . . paid by him with respect to employment." 26 U.S.C. " 3111(a), 3111(b), 3301. The Social Security tax provision, § 3111(a), contains a table prescribing tax rates applicable to "wages paid during" each year from 1984 onward (e.g., "In cases of wages paid during . . . 1990 or thereafter . . . [t]he rate shall be . . . 6.2 percent."). The Medicare tax provision, § 3111(b)(6), says "with respect to wages paid after December 31, 1985, the rate shall be 1.45 percent." And the FUTA tax provision, 26 U.S.C. § 3301 (1994 ed., Supp. IV), says the rate shall be "6.2 percent in the case of calendar years 1988 through 2007 . . . of the total wages (as defined in Section 3306(b)) paid by [the employer] during the calendar year."

$100,000 in FICA and FUTA taxes. The IRS appealed the district court's decision to the Sixth Circuit Court of Appeals. The IRS lost there. Not discouraged with consecutive losses, the IRS asked the Supreme Court to review the issue of the correct tax year.

The Ninth Inning

The U.S. Supreme Court stepped into the fray because the various federal circuit courts disagreed on the law. The Sixth Circuit had previously adopted the view that a settlement of back wages should be allocated to the period when the employer should have paid. Other circuits had concluded the opposite, back wages should be taxed in the year they are received.

The Internal Revenue Code says that taxes should be calculated based on the "wages paid during the year." But the text does not clearly answer the question notwithstanding the fact that the IRS had consistently followed the practice of calculating the taxes based upon the year in which the payment actually was made.

To a large extent, the problem of statutory construction was created by a prior U.S. Supreme Court decision, *Social Security Board v. Nierotko.* This case undercut the IRS's legal position. In 1946, the Court held that, for purposes of determining an employee's eligibility for Social Security benefits, which requires a certain number of calendar quarters of earned wages, back pay should be calculated as having been received in the calendar quarter in which the wages would have been earned, not when the back pay was actually paid.[9]

If this reasoning applied, the Indians would win. But the

9. Social Security Bd. v. Nierotko, 327 U.S. 358 (1946).

Court threw a breaking ball around the symmetry of the application argument. It distinguished *Nierotko* on the basis that it dealt with Social Security eligibility for benefits, and not with taxation of benefits. The fact that the language "wages paid" for benefit eligibility and the language for taxation was essentially the same did not mean that Congress meant the same thing:

> In all likelihood [the *Nierotko* holding] reflected concern that the benefits scheme created in 1939 would be disserved by allowing an employer's wrongdoing to reduce the quarters of coverage an employee would otherwise be entitled to claim toward eligibility. No similar concern underlies the tax provisions [involved in the Cleveland Indians case, even though both use the same statutory language].

The Indians made an interesting argument that employees could get the short end of the tax bat. It maintained, with considerable force of logic, that the IRS's reading of the tax code could be manipulated to the detriment of employees and to the benefit of employers:

> Under the Government's rule, an employee who should have been paid $100,000 in 1986, but is instead paid $50,000 in 1986 and $50,000 in backpay in 1994, would owe more tax than if she had been paid the full $100,000 due in 1986. Conversely, a wrongdoing employer who should have paid an employee $50,000 in each of five years covered by a $250,000 backpay award would pay only one year's worth of employment taxes (limited by the annual ceilings on taxable wages) in the year the award is actually paid.

In short, the IRS's rule appears to exempt some wages that

should be taxed and to tax some wages that should be exempt.

The Court's response is not especially reassuring. It reasoned that there are many anomalies in the tax code. It forthrightly recognized that sometimes the taxpayer is disadvantaged, while at other times the public fisc is disadvantaged.

Given that the text of the tax law did not answer the exact question, the Court reasoned that its role should be limited to deferring to the commissioner's tax regulations as long as they were reasonable. If a tax fairness problem exists with the IRS's approach, Congress should fix the tax law, which it had not done as evidenced by its inaction.

The IRS had consistently interpreted the tax law to require taxation of back wages according to the year the wages are actually paid, regardless of when those wages were earned or should have been paid. The Court also referred to revenue rulings, which construed back wages as taxable in the year they are actually paid. "Treasury regulations and interpretations long continued without substantial change, applying to unamended or substantially reenacted statutes, are deemed to have received congressional approval and have the effect of law."

In the end, the Court unanimously reversed the Sixth Circuit Court of Appeals, holding that back wages are subject to payroll (FICA and FUTA) taxes in the year they are paid, and not the year that those wages should have been paid. Consequently, the Sixth Circuit vacated its prior judgment and remanded the case to the district court to enter final judgment in favor of the United States.

The case has broad implications beyond baseball. The reasoning arguably applies to the taxation of lump-sum settlements of any labor disputes for back wages. The decision eliminates some confusion and kerfuffle in the tax law to which one can say loud and clear, "oyez."

Umpire's Ruling

The Luxury Tax

After the advent of the amateur draft and
before the advent of free agency, small-market
teams could hope to compete by drafting well and developing
and retaining strong players. Once players were free to make
their services available to the highest bidder (after sufficient
time in service), the field of play changed. Now the wealthiest
teams—usually those in the largest media markets, which
can command the most lucrative local television and radio
deals—are in a position to stockpile the best available
veterans.

Some professional sports leagues have addressed similar
problems by adopting salary caps that limit how much each
team can spend. Baseball's approach has been different.
Teams can spend as much as they want, but when they
exceed a certain predetermined payroll, they pay a "luxury
tax" on salaries above that level; in 2008, the tax kicks in
at an annual payroll of $155 million (calculated based on the
payroll for the 40-man roster). The tax is paid to the league.
In addition, a separate revenue-sharing plan redistributes
revenue from higher-revenue teams to lower-revenue teams.[1]

Neither of these plans entirely levels the playing field, but
teams have been able to overcome the payroll disadvantage.
The 2008 World Series winners, the Philadelphia Phillies, had
a payroll that ranked 13th of the 30 MLB teams; they defeated
the Tampa Bay Rays, whose payroll ranked next to last. The two
teams with the highest payrolls, the Yankees and the Tigers,
failed to make the playoffs; the Yankees' payroll easily exceeded
the payrolls of the Phillies and the Rays combined.[2]

---

1. http://www.blogs.payscale.com/salary_report_kris_cowan/2008/06/major-league-ba.html; http://espn.go.com/mlb/news/2002/0830/1425253.html.

2. http://www.blog.sportscolumn.com/story/2008/4/1/231932/3450/mlb/2008_MLB_Payrolls.

Fan Cries Foul

Jeffrey Swiecicki v. José Delgado,
463 F.3d 489 (6th Cir. 2006)[1]

Baseball fans are passionate about the game, and most are not shy about showing it. Although "you can't yell fire in a movie theater," unless there is in fact a fire, yelling at the players is part of the game. In fact, the home team often intentionally stirs the crowd's passion through scoreboard replays of the action, mascot antics, musical drumbeats, and the often-played chorus to "We Will Rock You," by Queen.

The judicial system sometimes is called upon when fans go overboard.[2] When this happens, fans are sometimes "kicked out of the game" by being ejected from the stadium or arrested for

---

1. *Available at* http://www.ca6.uscourts.gov/opinions.pdf/06a0355p-06.pdf (last visited Sept. 28, 2008).
2. Occasionally the umpires must settle matters when the fans go overboard. In 1974, for example, the public relations department for the Cleveland Indians had the bacchanalian idea to have a "10-cent beer night" to bring a crowd to see the team that no one would come see. Up to a point, it worked. Vast quantities of beer were sold to the thirsty crowd. But things turned into a public relations nightmare when drunken Cleveland fans swarmed the field and attacked Texas Rangers outfielder Jeff Burroughs. During the ensuing riot, rowdy fans brawled with players from both teams as well as with staff members. The umpires sent the fans packing for home by declaring a forfeit win by Texas.

allegedly violating the law.[3] But as *Swiecicki* illustrates, getting ejected or arrested may not be the end of the story.

In 2001, Jeffrey Swiecicki and several of his friends attended a baseball game between the Cleveland Indians and Toronto Blue Jays. The game was being played on the home turf of the Indians, Jacobs Field. During the game, Swiecicki proved himself to be an equal opportunity critic. He jeered the players on both teams, especially those close to his seat in left field.

José Delgado, an off-duty Cleveland city police officer, was working as a security guard to monitor fan behavior during the game. He was stationed at a tunnel near the leftfield bleachers where Swiecicki and his friends were enjoying the game and, as the court records show, a few beers. Although Delgado was officially off duty, he was wearing his police uniform and carrying his police department–issued weapons.

The fan-behavior rule at Jacobs Field provides:

> Persons using obscene or abusive language, or engaging in any other antisocial conduct offensive to those around them, will be asked by Cleveland Indians personnel to

---

3. During a 2002 baseball game between the Kansas City Royals and Chicago White Sox at "new" Comiskey Park (now U.S. Cellular Park), William Ligue, Jr., and his 15-year-old son went "crazy" while under the influence of drugs and alcohol. They rushed the field and assaulted Tom Gamboa, who was the first-base coach for the Royals. Both father and son were subsequently arrested and criminally charged with three counts of aggravated battery and one count of mob behavior. Both father and son were able to get off with only 30 months' probation, community service, and counseling. William, however, tangled with the law again in 2006. He is now in prison and up for parole in 2010.

In 2008, it was widely reported that alcohol was a factor in the death of Justin Hayes, a 25-year-old man, at Turner Field during a game between the Atlanta Braves and the New York Mets. During the eighth inning, Justin tried to slide down a railing when leaving the game. Tragically, he slipped over the railing and fell from the club level to the field level, a distance of about 150 feet. He was pronounced dead at Grady Memorial Hospital. The Braves stated that it was the first nonmedical fatality since moving into Turner Field in 1997.

cease this conduct. If the offensive conduct persists, those involved will be subject to ejection from the ballpark.

Although the fan-behavior rule prohibits obscene or abusive language, there is no rule against loud yelling, heckling, or booing. In fact, some may think it is all part of the fun.

Swiecicki led a group of fans in various heckles and cheers. He claimed that "almost the entire bleachers were yelling." Things heated up around the seventh inning. Delgado claimed that he heard Swiecicki yell "Russell Branyan, you suck" and "Branyan, you have a fat ass." Swiecicki admitted heckling Branyan, the Indians outfielder and third baseman. But he denied using profane language or being intoxicated.

Delgado contended that he saw Swiecicki with a beer in his hand at the time. Delgado told him to "cut it out." Swiecicki did not, however, respond. After motioning to Swiecicki to stop with no success, Delgado approached him and said that "we can either do this the easy way or the hard way." Apparently, it was the hard way.

Delgado grabbed Swiecicki's arm and shirt, placed him into the "escort position," and led him toward the tunnel to exit the stadium. Swiecicki repeatedly asked Delgado what he had done wrong, but Delgado did not answer. Things escalated when Swiecicki jerked his arm away to break from Delgado's grasp. Delgado responded by using an "arm bar" and wrestling him to the ground. Swiecicki hit his head on a door before falling to his knees. Once on the ground, Delgado pushed Swiecicki's face into the concrete and placed him under arrest. Police backup arrived, and Scott Swiecicki, Jeffrey's brother, was also arrested in the fracas.

Out of the Stadium and on to Court

Swiecicki was charged with aggravated disorderly conduct and with resisting arrest. He was found guilty by the Cleveland municipal court of the lesser-included offense of disorderly conduct and of resisting arrest. Not wanting his good name besmirched, Swiecicki appealed his convictions.

The Ohio Court of Appeals reversed his convictions.[4] It found that the evidence was insufficient to support the conviction of criminal disorderly conduct. The court reasoned that the words he used about Branyan "can hardly be perceived as offensive to ordinary sensibilities rising to the level of criminal disorderly conduct." It then added that "some in attendance may have even shared his sentiments." Ouch! This must have taken an emotional toll on Branyan.

The court also reversed the resisting arrest determination. An arrest is "lawful" when the surrounding circumstances give a reasonable police officer the belief that an offense is or has been committed. On the charge of resisting arrest, the court found that the prosecution failed to prove that Swiecicki had been lawfully arrested. Because the arrest was not lawfully established, the resisting arrest could not be sustained. But this was not the end of the Dickensian tale.

The Swiecicki brothers went to bat. They brought an action against Delgado for violating their civil rights in the U.S, District Court for the Northern District of Ohio. They alleged Delgado violated their constitutional rights to freedom of speech (count 1), freedom from arrest without probable case (count 2), freedom from excessive force (count 3), and freedom from malicious prosecution (count 4). They also alleged various state-based

---

4. City of Cleveland v. Swiecicki, 775 N.E.2d 899 (Ohio Ct. App. 2002). .

torts, including battery, assault, false imprisonment, false arrest, and malicious prosecution.

The federal claims were based on Section 1983. This section of Title 42 of the United States Code creates a cause of action for any person whose federal constitutional rights are violated by a "person" acting "under color of state law." Section 1983, which was enacted in 1871, provides the procedural mechanism for asserting a constitutional claim.

Section 1983 states:

> Every person who, under color of any statute, ordinance, regulation, custom, or usage, of any State or Territory or the District of Columbia, subjects, or causes to be subjected, any citizen of the United States or other person within the jurisdiction thereof to the deprivation of any rights, privileges, or immunities secured by the Constitution and laws, shall be liable to the party injured in an action at law, suit in equity, or other proper proceeding for redress, except that in any action brought against a judicial officer for an act or omission taken in such officer's judicial capacity . . .[5]

The statute does not expressly recognize any type of immunity. Nevertheless, some judicially recognized immunities exist to shield officials from liability for reasonable, albeit mistaken, judgments. Law enforcement officials generally enjoy "qualified immunity" provided they can show that they acted in "good faith."

The federal district court granted summary judgment in favor of Delgado. It reasoned that he was entitled to qualified immunity.

---

5. 42 U.S.C. § 1983 (2006).

On count 1, Swiecicki's First Amendment claim, the court found:

> A reasonable officer would not have thought that he or she was violating Jeffrey Swiecicki's constitutional right to free speech because there were grounds for the resisting arrest charge that involved physical action and had nothing to do with the content of Jeffrey's Swiecicki's speech. As a result, Officer Delgado will be granted qualified immunity on Jeffrey Swiecicki's First Amendment claim.

On count 2, the court found that a reasonable police officer could have believed that Swiecicki's loud and rowdy behavior provided "probable cause" to arrest him for aggravated disorderly conduct. Swiecicki's malicious prosecution claim, Count 4, failed for the same reason, namely, Delgado acted upon the reasonable belief that probable cause existed to arrest him.

Finally, the court found that count 3, the use of excessive force by Delgado, was barred by the statute of limitations that limits the time within which a plaintiff can file a lawsuit. The court also found that each of Scott Swiecicki's federal claims was barred by the statute of limitations.

Having found that the plaintiffs had no viable federal claims, the court then concluded that it no longer had the jurisdiction to consider plaintiffs' state-based claims, and thus dismissed them. The court said that the plaintiffs could have their state-based claims heard in state court. But that was not good enough for Swiecicki.

Jeffrey Swiecicki appealed to the U.S. Court of Appeals for the Sixth Circuit.

He had better luck there. The Sixth Circuit reversed the district court, and remanded the matter to it.

The Statute of Limitations

The Sixth Circuit first considered the district court's dismissal of count 3 as barred by the statute of limitations. Congress had not specified the time period (statute of limitations) within which a claim under Section 1983 must be brought by a plaintiff. Therefore, the federal courts "borrow" the state's statute of limitations governing personal injury actions, which in Ohio is two years.

In cases of excessive force, the time period typically begins to run at the time of arrest. Swiecicki filed his complaint against

Delgado more than two years after his arrest, but just more than one year after his conviction was reversed by the Ohio appellate court. The Sixth Circuit had to decide when the clock started to run on the claim of excessive force.

On the one hand, if the excessive force claim "would necessarily imply the invalidity of the criminal convictions," the clock would not start until a favorable termination of the underlying convictions occurred by the Ohio appellate court. On the other hand, if the excessive force claim was immediately cognizable—because it did not relate to the validity of the underlying arrest and conviction—then the two-year clock for the injury would run from the date of the arrest.

The Sixth Circuit concluded that the claim was timely. The claim of excessive force and the conviction for resisting arrest were related because, under Ohio law, an arrest is not lawful if the officer uses excessive force. If Swiecicki had brought his excessive-force claim before the Ohio appellate reversal, the Sixth Circuit said that the federal district court would have had to dismiss it. This meant, in the court's view, the clock began to run when the conviction was set aside by the Ohio appellate court.

Why this should be the case is not clear. Presumably, Swiecicki could prevail on an excessive force theory regardless of the disposition of the resisting arrest matter. Excessive force and resisting arrest are not inextricably linked. A jury might find that even if Swiecicki had improperly resisted arrest, Delgado still may have used excessive force. Notwithstanding these countervailing considerations, the Sixth Circuit found that the statute of limitations for the excessive force claim did not begin to run until the Ohio appellate court overturned Swiecicki's conviction. His claims could therefore be heard. But there was still the problem of immunity.

The Law of Qualified Immunity

The Sixth Circuit reversed the district court's grant of qualified immunity. On appeal, Swiecicki argued (1) that Delgado did not have probable cause to make the arrest as required by the Fourth Amendment and (2) Delgado violated his First Amendment rights based on the "content of his speech."

The court found that Delgado did not have probable cause to arrest Swiecicki for violating the disorderly conduct ordinance. The applicable ordinance required proof that Swiecicki engaged in "offensive or alarming behavior" and "that he was intoxicated." No one had actually complained about Swiecicki, and there was no evidence he was drunk. Thus, the record did not support the finding of disorderly conduct.

Turning to the offense of resisting arrest, which was the other charge, the Sixth Circuit found that the Cleveland ordinance required a lawful arrest on the underlying charge in order to sustain the conviction of resisting arrest. Delgado alleged Swiecicki jerked his arm away while being escorted from the stadium, whereas Swiecicki claimed his protest was verbal only. Because material facts were in dispute on the resisting arrest charge, the Sixth Circuit reversed the grant of qualified immunity.

The Sixth Circuit also analyzed Swiecicki's First Amendment claim. Delgado argued that the First Amendment did not apply to Jacobs Field, which he characterized as a private park maintained by a private entity. The ticket to attend the game was a license that could be revoked at will. The court summarily concluded "we are not persuaded."

The court reasoned that if Swiecicki was arrested based on the content of his heckling, which was his claim, then the arrest constituted a violation of his First Amendment rights. No evidence appeared in the record that his heckling rose to the level of "fighting words," which are not protected by the First Amendment. Moreover, no evidence was presented that other fans, even if they were offended by the jeers, were incited to become violent or that Branyan even heard his jeers. In short, the district court erred in basing its holding on disputed facts.

The Sixth Circuit found it was required to accept Swiecicki's version of the facts at the summary judgment stage. This meant that his verbal protests, in the court's view, were the only basis for Delgado's actions. Because Delgado lacked probable cause to arrest Swiecicki under these circumstances, and because Swiecicki's right to verbally protest his arrest was clearly established at the time of the arrest in question, it reversed the district court's grant of qualified immunity as it applied to Swiecicki's First Amendment claim.

Given that the ticket to the ball game stated that a fan could be removed if he used abusive language or engaged in other antisocial conduct, it is somewhat difficult to understand how a jury could conclude that Delgado's actions were in response to the content of his speech. Nevertheless, the court was not persuaded.

Granting summary judgment to Delgado on the basis of qualified immunity was incorrect. The case was remanded for further proceedings consistent with the Sixth Circuit's decision. Extra innings were required to settle the matter.

For Swiecicki to make a "federal case" out of being ejected from a game may well strike many as a colossal waste of judicial resources. A jury might well agree. But this case is one where the ultimate outcome is totally dependent on whose version of the facts one believes, which is up to the jury to decide. One thing, however, is certain. *Swiecicki v. Delgado* is sure to renew the debate about what constitutes appropriate fan behavior at a baseball game.

The Bartman Principle— There Are Worse Things from Fans than Foul Language

Long-suffering Chicago Cubs fans need no refresher on the saga of Steve Bartman. A 26-year-old employee of a human resources and consulting firm, Bartman was seated in foul territory down the left field line on October 14, 2003, in Wrigley Field as his beloved Cubbies battled the Florida Marlins in the National League Championship Series. Five outs from a victory that would have sent them to the World Series for the first time since 1945, the Cubs led the Marlins by a score of 3-0 when Luis Castillo lofted a pop fly to left. Cubs left-fielder Moises Alou reached into the seating area in an attempt to catch the ball, but Bartman reached for it too, preventing Alou from recording the second out of the inning. Visibly upset, Alou appeared to yell in Bartman's direction.

The Marlins went on to score eight runs in the inning and won the game. The next night, they beat the Cubs again to eliminate them from postseason play.[1]

After Bartman's action, the Cubs argued that Castillo should have been called out under the rule regarding spectator interference. That rule provides that "[s]pectator interference occurs when a spectator reaches out of the stands, or goes on the playing field, and touches a live ball."[2] The rules further provide that, "When there is spectator interference with any thrown or batted ball, the ball shall be dead at the moment of interference and the umpire shall impose such penalties as in his opinion will nullify the act of interference."[3] The umpires concluded that Bartman had not reached out of the stands to attempt to catch the ball and so the rule did not apply.[4] Fans can get out of the way of players reaching into the stands if

Umpire's Ruling (continued)

they wish, but the rules do not require it. Accordingly, the umpires imposed no penalty on the Marlins. But Cubs fans imposed a penalty on Bartman. They showered him with obscenities and debris as he was escorted from the stadium under police protection.

1. http://www.en.wikipedia.org/wiki/Steve_Bartman.
2. Rule 2.00(d).
3. Rule 3.16.
4. http://www.redorbit.com/news/general/25204/marlins_cubs_to_play_game_7_tonight/index.html.

About the Authors

John "Jack" H. Minan is a professor of law at the University of San Diego and a baseball fan. He is the author of the American Bar Association's popular *The Little Green Book of Golf Law— The Real Rules of the Game of Golf.*

Jack has been associate dean for Academic Affairs, Acting Dean of Summer Programs, and the Director of USD's International and Comparative Law Programs at Trinity College, Dublin, at Magdalen College, Oxford, and in Florence, Italy. He has authored or coauthored seven books, four contributions to books, more than forty scholarly articles, and numerous published reports and proceedings.

Jack has a B.S. from the University of Louisville, a M.B.A. from the University of Kentucky, and a J.D. from the University of Oregon. He has completed postgraduate course work in Operations Analysis at American University. Jack has practiced admiralty law as a trial attorney with the U.S. Department of Justice, and has qualified as an expert witness on matters involving Land Use Planning and Real Property.

Jack served as a gubernatorial appointee to the California Regional Water Quality Control Board from 1999 to 2006, and served six consecutive one-year terms as its chairman. Professor Minan served on the Board of Governors of the Southern California Wetlands Recovery Project, an organization consisting of seventeen state and federal agencies. He has been on the Board of the San Diego River Conservancy, a state agency dedicated to the acquisition and management of public lands in the San Diego Region, and served as its vice-chairman.

Jack is active with the American Bar Association. He has served on the Council and as the chairman of the Environmental Law Committee, State and Local Government Section. He also has been active with the Section Environment, Energy, and Resources.

Author's note

Kevin Cole is the Dean of the University of San Diego School of Law. He joined the faculty in 1987 and specialized in the areas of criminal law, criminal procedure, and evidence before becoming dean in 2005.

Index

A

Alex Popov v. Patrick Hayashi 87-93
  See ownership of Barry Bonds's
  73rd home run ball 87
Alou, Moises 225
antitrust exemption of baseball, 38–45, 49–57
  business of baseball, defined 42
  Federal Baseball Club of Baltimore v. National League 39–45
  Federal League
    creation of 40
    dissolution of 40
    peace agreement with MLB 40
  Federal League, Baltimore club
    filing of antitrust suit against MLB 40
  Holmes, Oliver Wendell
    opinion on MLB antitrust violation 42
  Hooper v. California 43
  National and American Leagues
    1903 agreement between 40
  reserve clause. *See also.* 50
  Sherman Antitrust Act 39–41
Arizona Diamondbacks 205
Atlanta Braves 206
Avila, José 174
Avila v. Citrus Community College District
  See beanballs. 169

B

ballparks, building of
  See Petco Park, building of
Bartman, Steve 225
baseball memorabilia, market value of 93
baseball rules
  appeals 84

arguing balls and strikes calls 24
assignment of player contract 53
balks 58
ball lodged in paraphernalia 36
balls hitting players 125
ball in play, declaration of 59
bats, characteristics of 152
batting helmets 180
batting order, submission of 202
batting out of order 136
catch, determination of 104
catcher's interference 148
causation 165
collusion on the field 46
dead ball 59
definition of a catch 104
delaying tactics 84
doctored bats 189
election of remedies 148
fielder obstruction 165
foul tip lodged in catcher's mask 36
glove thrown at batted ball 36
gloves, wearing of 36
hidden ball trick 59
incapacitation of player 114
injuries to players 114
intentionally dropped line drive or fly ball 58
intentionally throwing at batter 173
interference 12
luxury tax 212
manager visitation of pitcher 202
material applied to bats 184
pitcher intentionally throwing at batter 167
postponement of game 202
prohibited speech 24
prohibition against player fraternization 46

protest withdrawal 84
protecting the batter 180
readiness of batter 84
resolving points not covered
in the rules 12
Rule 1.10 152
Rule 1.10(a) 189
Rule 1.10(b) 184
Rule 1.10(c) 190
Rule 1.11 68
Rule 1.14 36
Rule 1.15 36
Rule 2.00 36, 104
Rule 2.00(d). 225
Rule 3 52
Rule 3.03 202
Rule 3.16 165
Rule 3.09 46
Rule 3.16. 225
Rule 4.01(c) 202
Rule 4.01(d) 202
Rule 4.06(a)(3) 167
Rule 4.15 84
Rule 4.19 84
Rule 5.02 59
Rule 5.09(g) 36
Rule 5.10(c) 114
Rule 5.11 59
Rule 6.02 84
Rule 6.02(b) 136
Rule 6.05 58
Rule 6.06(d) 189
Rule 6.09 148
Rule 7.05(b)-(e) 167
Rule 7.05(c), 7.05(e) 36
Rule 7.06(a)-(b) 165
Rule 8.02(b) 167
Rule 8.02(d) 167, 173
Rule 8.02b 148
Rule 8.04 84
Rule 8.05 58
Rule 8.06 202
Rule 9 53
Rule 9.01(c) 12

Rule 9.02(a) 24
spectator interference 225
strike zone, changing definition
of 169
tampering 52
team branding 68
uniform, characteristics of 68
uniform contract 52
baseball strike of 1981 130
beanballs 169–79
Avila, José
injured by pitch in college
game 174
*Avila v. Citrus Community
College District* 169–79
baseball rules against 172
brushback pitch, defined 170
Chapman, Ray 170
criminal prosecution for 171
defined 170
"headhunters," pitchers known
as 171
penalties for throwing 173
retaliation 172
strike zone, defined 169
suit filed by college player
hazardous recreational
activity 176
inherent-risk analysis 178
intentional tort of battery
and for negligence 175
primary assumption of risk 177
public entity tort liability 175
Benejam, Alyssia Maribel 108
Benejam v. Detroit Tigers, Inc.
See stadium liability for spectator
injury
Berra, Yogi 151
Black Sox scandal 15
Bonds, Barry 87–93 104, 180
criminal indictment for alleged
steroid use 93
setting single-season home run
record 88

Boston Red Sox 3, 8, 68

Branyan, Russell 217

breach of contract 139–48

baseball games preempted by
NFL games 142

contract, ESPN and MLB

basics of 140

ESPN's right of preemption 141

failure to seek redress 142

no-waiver clause 141

election of remedies 143–44

pursuit of inconsistent
remedies 145

*ESPN, Inc. v. Office of the
Commissioner of Baseball* 139

MLB refusal of preemption
request 143

MLB termination of agreement
with ESPN 143

refusal to honor telecast
contract 140

self-help, ESPN claim of 145

Brett, George 183–88. *Also see*
trademark stockpiling.

pine tar incident 183

Brett, Jeremy 160

Brett v. Hillerich & Bradsby Co.

See pitcher safety and metal bats

brushback pitches

See beanballs 169

C

California State University,
Northridge 155

"Casey at the Bat" 135

Castillo, Luis 225

catcher's mask, invention of

See patent law

*CBC Distribution and Marketing,
Inc. v. Major League Baseball
Advanced Media, L.P.*

See fantasy baseball

*Central Manufacturing, Inc. v.
George Brett and Brothers*

See trademark stockpiling 183

Chapman, Ray 170, 180

Chicago Cubs 4, 59, 189, 225

Chicago White Stockings 28, 35

chin music

See beanballs 169

Citrus College 174

City of San Diego v. Dunkl 76

See also Petco Park, building of

Clemens, Roger 171

Cleveland Indians 155, 170, 205, 216

Cleveland Spiders 205

Colbern, Mike 130

Colorado Rockies 62, 151

Consumer Product Safety Act 160

Coolbaugh, Mike 151

Correa, Dominic 155

*Crane v. Kansas City Baseball
& Exhibition Co.*

See stadium liability for
spectator injury

Currie v. City of San Diego 78

See also Petco Park, building of

D

Delgado, José

See disorderly conduct, fan
arrest for

Detroit Tigers 108, 212

disorderly conduct, fan arrest for
215–24

Delgado, José

arrest of fan 216

qualified immunity for 219

Jacobs Field 216

fan-behavior rule 216

law of qualified immunity 223

Swiecicki, Jeffrey

appeal of conviction 218

arrest of 216

conviction of 218

excessive force claim 222

suit claiming civil rights
violation 218

Donchez, Robert 61–67
See service mark
Donchez v. Coors Brewing Co.
See service mark
Drysdale, Don 171

E

*ESPN, Inc. v. Office of the
Commissioner of Baseball*
See breach of contract

F

Fairly, Ron 172
fantasy baseball 15–23
*CBC Distribution and Marketing,
Inc. v. Major League Baseball
Advanced Media, L.P.* 15–23
CBC Distribution and Marketing
baseball players information,
use of 19
fees paid to 18
Advanced Media, suit
against 18
First Amendment rights of
baseball fans 21
breach of material contractual
obligation 23
MLBPA charge of licenses
agreement violation 22
functioning of 17
Major League Baseball Advanced
Media, L.P. 18
prize money 17
right of publicity 19
alleged violation of 19
commercial advantage
requirement 20
defined 19
symbol-of-identity requirement
20
right to operate without paying a
licence fees 23
sale of fantasy sports products 17
*Federal Baseball Club of Baltimore
v. National League*
See antitrust exemption of baseball

Federal Insurance Contributions
Act 207
Federal Unemployment Tax Act 207
Fenway Park 6
Field of Dreams 15
Fish, Alan
See spectator injury, negligent
medical assistance
*Fish v. Los Angeles Dodgers
Baseball Club, et al.*
See spectator injury, negligent
medical assistance
Flood, Curt 49–57. *Also see* reserve
clause.
challenge to reserve clause 49-57
Curt Flood Act, passage of 55
legacy of 57
request for free agency 50
Flood v. Kuhn et al.
See reserve clause
Florida Marlins 225

G

Gossage, Rich "Goose" 183

H

Hayashi, Patrick
See ownership of Barry Bonds's
73rd home run ball
Henderson, J. Bruce
See Petco Park, building of
Herman v. Admit One 11
Hillerich & Bradsby Company 156
Holmes, Oliver Wendell
dynamic nature of the law 45
opinion in baseball antitrust
case 42
Hooper v. California 43

I

Internal Revenue Service 207

J

Jackson, "Shoeless" Joe 15
Jacobs Field 216

Jeffrey Swiecicki v. José Delgado
  See disorderly conduct, fan arrest for
Johnson, Randy 12, 171, 205
Jones, Glen E. 120

K

Kansas City Royals 151, 183
Kuhn, Bowie 50

L

Lainer v. City of Boston
  See ticket scalping
Levine v. Brooklyn Nat'l League Baseball Club, Inc.
  See ticket scalping
Los Angeles Dodgers 88, 117,172

M

Mackay, Jack 157–59
MacPhail, Lee 184
Mailhot, Jerry 74
Major League Umpires Association v. American League
  See umpires, mass resignation of
Major League Umpires Association 196
Marichal, Juan 172
Martin, Billy 183
Martínez, Pedro 171
Mays, Carl 170
McClelland, Tim 183
McDonald v. Santa Fe Trail Transp. Co. 133
McDougald, Gil 155
McGwire, Mark 87
Merrill, Durwood 196
metal bats
  See pitcher safety and metal bats 151
Miller, Marvin 57
Mitchell, George 93
  report on steroid use in baseball 93
MLB Network, launch of 147

Montgomery, Bob 180
Moores, John
  See Petco Park, building of
Moran, Richard Alan 130
Moran v. Selig
  See reverse discrimination

N

National Baseball Hall of Fame 183
National Collegiate Athletic Association 156
National Federation of State High School Association 161
National High School Baseball Coaches Association 162
National Sporting Goods Association 152
Negro leagues 129
New York Mets 206
New York Yankees 3, 51, 68, 72, 170, 183, 205, 212
Nuzzo, Jim 193

O

O'Nora, Brian 151
ownership of Barry Bonds's 73rd home run ball 87–93
  Alex Popov v. Patrick Hayashi 87–93
  baseball memorabilia, market value of 93
  control of the ball, determining 90
  Gray's rule 90
  Hayashi, Patrick 89
    fairness claim 91
  incidental contact 91
  Popov, Alex 88
    trespass to chattel suit filed 89
  qualified pre-possessory interest 92
  qualified right to possession 91
  tax consequences of selling the ball 92
  trespass to chattel
    defined 89

P

Pac-10 athletic conference 155
Padres L.P. v. Henderson
  See Petco Park, building of
patent law 27–30
  catcher's mask, invention of 28
    purpose of 32
    suit charging patent
      infringement 32
  doctrine of equivalents 33
  infringement 30
    claims, proof of 30
  infringement claims 30
  invention, patentabilty of 30
  principles of 29
  prior public use 32
  Thayer v. Spaulding 27–30
payroll tax litigation 205–11
  applicable tax rate, determination
    of 207
  overpayment of Social Security
    and unemployment taxes 206
  owner collusion to depress player
    salaries 206
  statutory construction 209
  suit seeking tax refund 207
  *Social Security Board v.
    Nierotko* 209
  *United States v. Cleveland
    Indians Baseball Company*
    205-11
People v. Shepard
  See ticket scalping
Perry, Gaylord 184
Petco Park, building of 72–81
  appropriation ordinance for 75
  ballot measure on 74
  City of San Diego v. Dunkl 76
  Currie v. City of San Diego 78
  environmental impact report,
    need for 75
  financial obligations of city 75
  initiative petition seeking
    termination of stadium 76

J. Bruce Henderson, opposition
  to 72
  lawsuits filed against 73
  Mailhot I 74
    suit to block public vote on 74
  Mailhot II 76
    challenge to city's actions on
      stadium construction 76
  Mailhot III
    charges of violating city charter
      provisions 76
  Padres L.P. v. Henderson 72–81
    Strategic Lawsuits Against
      Public Participation (SLAPP)
      79–81
    tort of malicious prosecution 81
  Skane v. City of San Diego 78
  voter approval of 75
Philadelphia Phillies 50, 212
pitcher intentionally throwing at
  hitter
  See beanballs. 170
pitcher safety and metal bats 151–68
  American Legion pitcher, death
    of 151
  Brett, Jeremy
    high school player injured by
      batted ball 160
  Brett v. Hillerich & Bradsby Co.
    151–63
  Consumer Product Safety Act
    petition regarding non-wood
      bats 160
  hit-ball velocity 153
  injured college player, suit filed
    156–59
    allowing use of a dangerous
      bat 156
    assumption of risk 157
    bat as cause of accident 158
    bat as defective 158
    elimination of risk,
      consequences of 159
    increased risk posed by bat 159
    motions for summary judgment
      157

metal bat use, controversy surrounding 160

metal bats, risks associated with 152

National Federation of State High School Association 161

National Sporting Goods Association

    wood bats, sale of 152

New York City ordinance on metal bats 161

    USA Baseball v. City of New York 162

    violation of due process and equal protection 162

performance level of metal bats 153

pitcher's style of delivery 154

Sanchez, Andrew

    injured by batted ball in college game 155

Pittsburgh Athletic Co. v. KQV Broadcasting Co. 147

Polo Grounds 170

Popov, Alex

    See ownership of Barry Bonds's 73rd home run ball

Q

Quisenberry, Dan 185

R

reserve clause 49–57

    challenge to

        constraint of personal freedom 50

        Toolson v. New York Yankees 51

    Congressional action

    Curt Flood Act, passage of 55

    Curt Flood challenge to 50

    description of 52

    Flood v. Kuhn et al. 49–57

    Kuhn, Bowie 50

    reserve system 52

    uniform player's contract, provisions of 53

reverse discrimination 129–35

    adverse employment action 133

    Civil Rights Act, Title VII 131

    claim of disparate treatment 132

    Colbern, Mike, claim of 130

    Equal Employment Opportunity Commission 131

    favorable treatment, proof of 134

    four-season rule 130

    Moran v. Selig 129–35

    Negro League

        MLB benefit plans for 134

    pension benefits vesting 130

    Selig, Bud 131

right of publicity 65–68. *See also* service mark

    as intellectual property right 65

    infringement, determining 67

    Restatement (Third) of Unfair Competition 66

    violation of 65–66

        cause of action 66

Rio Hondo Community College 174

Rivera, Mariano 205

Roberts, John 195

Robinson, Jackie 129

    integration of baseball 129

Ruth, Babe 3, 152

S

Sample, Joe 185

San Diego Padres 72–81

San Francisco Giants 88

Sanchez, Andrew

    See pitcher safety and metal bats

Sanchez v. Hillerich & Bradsby Co.

    See pitcher safety and metal bats

Score, Herb 155

Selig, Bud 93, 131, 139, 196–198

service mark 61–67

    defined 63

    descriptive-secondary meaning 64

Donchez, Robert
  suit against Coors, Inc. 61
  right of publicity. *See also*
  Donchez v. Coors Brewing Co.
  61–67
  generic 63
  protection, qualification for 63
  purpose of 63
Sherman Antitrust Act 39–41
Silverman v. Major League
Baseball Player Relations
Comm., Inc. 194
Skane v. City of San Diego
  See Petco Park, building of
Social Security Board v. Nierotko
  See payroll tax litigation
Society for the Prevention of
Trademark Abuse, LLC 188
Sosa, Sammy 189
Spaulding, Albert Goodwill
  See patent law
spectator injury and negligent
medical assistance 117-24
  cause-in-law 118
  duty of care 118
    breach of 118
  Fish, Alan
    Children's Hospital, treatment
    at 121
    injury at ballpark 119
    treatment at ballpark
    emergency first-aid station 120
  intervening act by a third
  person 118
  lawsuit filed by Fish family 122
    essential legal principles
    covered in jury instructions 124
  principles of negligence and
  apparent authority 117
  proximate cause 118
spectator injury, stadium liability for
  See stadium liability for spectator
  injury
Springer, Dennis 88

St. Louis Cardinals 49
stadium liability for spectator injury
107–13
  Benejam, Alyssia Maribel
    injured at ballpark 108
    suit for injury sustained at
    ballpark 108
  Benejam v. Detroit Tigers,
  Inc. 107
  Crane v. Kansas City Baseball
  & Exhibition Co. 108
  duty to warn 110
  inviter-invitee principles 110
  legal duty to protect against
  harm 107
  limited-duty rule 110
    inconsistent with duty to
    warn 111
  special "baseball rule" 110
  standard of care 109
steroid use in baseball 93
  Barry Bonds, suspicion of 93
  Mitchell Report on 93
Stoller, Leo 186
strike zone, changing definition
of 169
Swiecicki, Jeffrey
  See disorderly conduct, fan
  arrest for
Swiecicki, Scott
  See disorderly conduct, fan
  arrest for

T

Tampa Bay Rays 212
Thayer, Ernest 135
Thayer, Fred W.
  See patent law
Thayer v. Spaulding
  See patent law
ticket resale as business venture
9–11
  Herman v. Admit One 11
  licensing of broker 9
  service charges 10